# Making Formative
# Assessment Work

# Making Formative Assessment Work

## Effective Practice in the Primary Classroom

*Kathy Hall and Winifred M. Burke*

Open University Press

Open University Press
McGraw-Hill Education
McGraw-Hill House
Shoppenhangers Road
Maidenhead
Berkshire
England
SL6 2QL

email: enquiries@openup.co.uk
world wide web: www.openup.co.uk

First published 2003

A catalogue record for this book is available from the British Library.

ISBN 0335 213790 (pb) 0335 213804 (hb)

Library of Congress Cataloging-in-Publication Data
CIP data applied for

Typeset by YHT Ltd, London
Printed in Great Britain by MPG Books Ltd, Bodmin, Cornwall

*To Rita Kavanagh and to the memory of Mary and Edward Burke*

# Contents

# Contents

# Acknowledgements

Thanks to the two teachers and pupils involved in the case study reported in Chapters 3 and 4. Thanks also to the many other teachers and pupils who we have met since we began researching this topic. They have informed and modified our thinking about 'assessment for learning'. Thanks to Patricia Murphy for the inspiration she provided, through her writing, for the case study reported in Chapter 7. We wish to express our gratitude to Taylor and Francis for permission to reproduce, in Chapter 13, material already published (Hall K. and Harding A., 2002, Level Descriptions of Teacher Assessment: Towards a community of assessment practice, Educational Research 40, 1, 1–16). We also acknowledge the Economic and Social Research Council for funding the research on which that work was based. We are grateful to the Department of Education and Science, Republic of Ireland, for permission to reproduce, in Chapter 6, material from *Oideas* (K. Hall 2001, Reading assessment as an instrument of pedagogic reform, *Oideas*, 49: 39–55). We would like to thank Jacqui Dean for helpful references and material for Chapter 10. Thanks to Shona Mullen and Melanie Smith at Open University Press, especially for Melanie's patient responses to questions and her good advice as the completion date drew near. Thanks to Tom Smith and Olive Driver for providing valuable backing at all stages in the production of this book.

# Acknowledgements

# Introduction

What we know about assessment has advanced considerably over the past decade or so. One insight that is increasingly recognized, particularly by researchers and practitioners, is the importance of formative assessment. Evidence from teacher effectiveness studies shows that assessment that is learner-centred – i.e. assessment that is geared to helping the learner make progress – is a major characteristic of successful teachers' practice. The demands of the standards set by the Teacher Training Agency (TTA) for student teachers and the expectations of the Office for Standards in Education (Ofsted) for schools mean that teachers are now being urged to incorporate formative assessment into their classroom practice much more explicitly and consciously than they did in the past.

However, the available evidence suggests that policies have underestimated the complexity of this kind of assessment and that teachers, and especially student teachers, find it difficult to do. The rationale for this book stems from that recognition. The book explains and exemplifies formative assessment in practice in the primary school. It explores formative assessment by attending to the reality and complexity of classroom life. Drawing on incidents and case studies from primary settings, it describes and analyses how teachers in regular classrooms use formative assessment to promote their pupils' learning. It grapples with the barriers to, as well as the factors that enhance, the use of formative assessment. It explains the case for formative assessment with reference to what we know about the way learning occurs as well as with reference to the kind of learning that matters increasingly in school, and in life more generally.

We have sought to bring together issues of theory and practice in such a way as to encourage student teachers and practitioners to apply their understanding to their own teaching context and to consider more critically their own and others' policies and practices. We are seeking to equip the reader with a sophisticated grasp of assessment issues – specifically, issues in formative assessment, and how they relate to the promotion of pupil learning. We aim, particularly, to support the reader in understanding what counts as formative assessment and what practices are likely to promote high quality learning. Throughout we try to make clear the assumptions underlying our interpretations of classroom events since this, it seems to us, is an important element in understanding and developing a rationale for professional practice. We do not seek to impose our perspectives about learning (about say literacy, art or science) on our readers. Rather we see our role as inviting our readers to develop their own critical perspectives in a way that enables them better to explain and justify their own professional decisions.

The book links assessment and learning throughout. It begins with a discussion of recent thinking about learning and by identifying some key principles and concepts that assessment practice has to take on board. It considers the current policy on assessment generally and on formative assessment particularly. The first two chapters set the scene for the rest of the book. However, these chapters do more than just describe contemporary themes in learning and assessment. They also, perhaps inevitably, provide an account of our take on learning. We consider this to be highly relevant to any discussion of assessment since one's perspective on the latter is informed by one's stance on learning. In making explicit our position on learning we are inviting you, the reader, to consider and develop your own perspective.

The first two chapters are followed by accounts from the field covering a wide range of themes, subject areas and assessment contexts. For example, feedback to the learner, teacher assessment, self- and peer assessment and the location of power in the assessment enterprise are themes that are dealt with separately and are then revisited in the context of various curricular areas. Curriculum areas addressed include literacy, numeracy, science, art and design, and history. Learning how to learn and learning dispositions are themes that are also addressed, especially with reference to the early years of school. The final chapter could be read as being more about summative than formative assessment. In fact it is about both. It is concerned with the way assessment information may be used for different purposes and here we consider how summative assessments can be used in a formative way. The conclusion speculates about the future status of formative assessment in policy and practice and briefly considers some issues for schools arising from the chapters.

# 1  Learning and Assessment

## Introduction

This first chapter discusses key concepts in current thinking on learning and assessment. It starts by discussing important themes in contemporary learning theory. We locate ourselves theoretically as we outline these ideas about learning. We begin to describe a view of assessment that logically follows from our perspective on learning and this is picked up and extended in relation to domains of learning throughout the remaining chapters of the book. This chapter seeks to provide an analytical framework within which readers can evaluate their own learning and assessment decisions as well as those taken by their school, local education authority (LEA) and at national level. Before we can sensibly discuss what model of assessment we should use to enhance learning, we have to consider what we know about learning itself.

## Learner as sense-maker

The idea that learning is a mechanistic process of breaking down knowledge into smaller units for pupils to digest mentally is now obsolete. We now know that:

- learning occurs through active intellectual engagement on the part of the learner;
- it is always in a context and involves constructing meaning; and
- it involves linking new knowledge with previous understanding.

These three characteristics of learning are well explained by von Glasersfeld (1989) in an essay entitled, 'Learning as a constructive activity', by Wood (1988) in the book, *How Children Think and Learn* and by Bruner (1996) in *The Culture of Education*. To learn, says von Glasersfeld, means to draw conclusions from experience and to act accordingly. The expectation that we can control experience is founded on the assumption that we can detect patterns in our experiences and that future experience will, to some extent, conform to these patterns. The recalling and assessing of patterns and similarities and the decisions as to what is to be considered different in any given experience are all our own doing. As learners, we make our own sense and build our own connections no matter how brilliant the teacher. We do not simply discover things. Each learner interprets, makes sense of and builds their own unique representation of what was taught because it gets connected to each learner's unique set of prior understandings (Good and Brophy 1994).

The context of teaching and learning is important. Context includes the learner's construction or interpretation of the whole learning scenario and does not merely refer to the physical features of the setting or the task – including an assessment task. Learners make sense of situations for themselves and each learner will make their own 'sense'. Consider, for example, children's responses to an adventure story where the heroes overcome multiple hurdles to achieve their goals: while all might think about the same storyline and sequence of events, one reader might remember and think about the sense of achievement felt by the characters; another might think about the text as a story about teamwork; and another about how the shared adventure seals the bonds of friendship and so on. Although all were exposed to the same narrative as written by its author or told by the teacher, they reconstruct it for themselves in slightly different ways.

The teacher can enhance (or hinder) the process of constructing interpretations of our experience. To make sense of a given collection of experiences means to have organized or constructed them in a manner that allows us to make more or less reliable predictions (von Glasersfeld 1989). But the way we have constructed them is but one viable way – there may be other possible constructions, other possible 'truths'. Von Glasersfeld views knowledge and competence as products of the individual's conceptual organization and the individual's experience, and therefore the role of the teacher is no longer to dispense 'truth' but rather to guide the learner in the conceptual organization of their experience. From this it follows that teaching demands that the teacher constructs a model of the learner's concepts and knowledge as well as models of where learning is heading. Von Glasersfeld refers to two perspectives the teacher needs to have: 'on the one hand, an adequate idea of where the student is and, on the other, an adequate idea of the destination' (p. 17).

The model of learning described above is one of the more or less lone learner actively making connections between the familiar and the less familiar, between new information and existing networks of prior knowledge. To learn well, the learner benefits from the chance to apply the new learning. It assumes that before ideas become usable for interpreting new situations, for solving problems, for thinking and reasoning, and learning generally, learners must have the opportunity to play around with what they have learned in order to make it their own. They need the chance to question it, elaborate it and apply it in purposeful contexts, especially everyday life situations. Otherwise, the knowledge may remain inert – recallable only when cued by teacher questioning or by a test.

## Learner-plus-surround

However, an individual's sense-making or representation of an experience or what was taught is 'situated'. This means it is mediated by social partners, by taken for granted ways of doing things, and by tools like language and technology. Gavriel Salomon (1993: xiii) puts it as follows: 'People appear to think in conjunction or partnership with others and with the help of culturally provided tools and implements'. This is to recognize the symbolic nature of knowledge and thought – that knowledge is based on agreed-upon beliefs about the world, based in turn on human beings' interactions within that world. Meaning emerges from social interactions.

The idea of social interactions and classroom discourse appeals to us. The idea of discourse, in particular, highlights the way that knowledge is constructed and exchanged in the moment-by-moment interactions in classrooms. Discourse is related to fundamental issues of power, such as who talks about what and in what ways, as well as issues of what constitutes knowledge and evidence (Graue 1993; Hall 2002).

The idea that knowledge is based on people's agreed-upon beliefs about the world and their interactions within that world originated in the writings of the Soviet psychologist Lev Vygotsky (1978) but have been taken up and developed by several others over recent decades (e.g. Bruner 1996; Lee and Smagorinsky 2000). Vygotsky talks about 'socio-constructivism' and Bruner describes his theory as 'cultural psychology'. For convenience, but mostly because we think his development of Vygotskian thinking over recent decades is especially insightful and brimming with implications for assessment, we take Bruner's research as an important theoretical base here.

Culture is about the way we make meanings, the way we assign meanings to things in different settings. Culture is a result of people's histories, experiences and efforts, and it also shapes those histories, experiences and efforts. This is a crucial idea, for its major implication is that learning and thinking are always situated, always in a context and always dependent on the use of person-made tools or resources. And the tool of all person-made tools is surely language. Language is the primary symbol system that allows us to shape meaning – it gives our thoughts shape and expression, yet it also shapes our very thoughts in the process. This leads to the conclusion that learning is inherently social, even when others are not physically present. Even reading a book alone involves the reader in a written code developed through long periods of use by other people and of course what the reader brings to the book has been influenced by the thinking of others and the previous social contexts in which the reader has been (Au 1997; Lee and Smagorinsky 2000).

Bruner makes the important point that while nothing is culture-free, neither are individuals mere reflections of their culture. The interaction between the individual and the culture gives rise to human thought having 'a communal cast' on the one hand and having an 'unpredictable richness on the other' (Bruner 1996: 14). This gives rise to subjectivity – one's personal take on a situation or event – which in turn gives rise to the need to negotiate, share and communicate our meanings to others in the community. But, as Bruner observes, humans have a sophisticated gift for coming to know the minds of others in their community – he calls this intersubjectivity – whether through language or other signs like gestures.

So children, Bruner argues, are especially good at tuning in to what he calls the 'folkways' they see around them. They are predisposed to assimilate the practices and activities of their parents and their peers in the community. They appear to be willing apprentices to their more adept peers. On the other hand, adults, and arguably any knowledgeable people in the culture, appear to have a disposition to demonstrate performance for the benefit of the novice. They appear to be willing mentors. Knowledgeable members of the culture assist others in learning. The notion of apprenticeship becomes important. It flags the learner as active, not passive, in a community of people who support, challenge and guide development.

On the grounds that children are active learners, Bruner suggests that teachers have to be interested in determining what learners think they are doing and their reasons for doing it. He also says 'a cultural approach emphasises that the child only gradually comes to appreciate that she is acting not directly on the world but on beliefs about that world' (1996: 49). Learning then, like any social activity, involves a set of cultural practices that are embedded within webs of relationships. This is a stance that sees the learner as a thinker, as knowledgeable and as having agency. It is a stance that sees the process of learning as a social one as well as a cognitive one, as a process involving motivational and emotional dimensions as well as intellectual and academic ones. In our view we ignore the affective aspect of learning at our peril.

This position on learning takes the classroom itself as a context and a culture in its own right – i.e. it has its own system of socially made beliefs, values and ways of doing things and that these in turn guide people's thoughts, feelings and behaviours (Au 1997). The classroom or school or home or community is a community of practice with its own ways of learning and demonstrating learning. A community in this context refers to a shared set of social practices and goals, to the patterns and habits of behaviour and thinking on the part of groups of people – it refers to ways of being in the world.

In this regard it is worth noting that problems that some learners may encounter in schools lie not so much in the acquisition of cognitive skills, but in becoming accustomed to the specific tasks and activities required by the school (see Cole 1990). If you see learning as a social practice, then you are likely to see teaching as apprenticing children into the discourses and social practices of literate, scientific, mathematical (and so on) communities. Thus language, social interaction and the social situatedness of learning are of paramount importance. Dialogue and discussion, the exchange of views and the negotiation of meanings are all fundamental aspects of learning. In this conception of learning pupils are encouraged in 'negotiating and re-negotiating meaning' (Bruner 1990: 123). The central point is that human beings learn in the course of participating purposefully in joint activity. With assistance from more expert others they master the use of the tools (including meaning-making tools like talk and writing), materials and practices that are part and parcel of achievement and success in the valued activities in question.

Hence our heading 'learner-plus-surround' which refers to the idea that learning doesn't just happen in our heads but in networks of relationships. The 'surround', which refers to the physical, social and symbolic resources outside the person, participates in learning as well as the person – the surround is a tool for thinking. As Margaret Carr (2001: 8) observes 'The surround does part of the thinking, and holds part of the learning'. In an important sense then, learners engage in activities, they change those activities and they are also changed *by* the activities. We can talk about learning therefore as a transaction or as involving a reciprocal relationship between the environment and the mind.

Key features of this stance on learning, to which we subscribe, can be summarized as follows:

- meanings and interpretations are co-constructed through discussion and activity;

- everyone has a contribution to make: authority for constructed knowledge does not lie solely with the teacher or in a text – it resides also with the learners, their relationships with each other and the activities they are engaged in, plus the way they are expected to view these activities;
- learners strive to make sense of new ideas by relating them to their prior knowledge and to the expectations that they construe, from the task or activity, about their role;
- learning anything, say literacy, is about becoming someone who is able to participate successfully in that community of practitioners (e.g. readers, writers, listeners, speakers in this class, this school, etc.) and becoming someone who is able to use the tools and resources associated with that particular community of practitioners;
- learning involves acquiring new ways of participating, and with those new ways come new identities for the learner.

## So what kind of teaching?

One of the implications of what we know about learning is that interventions to help learners become more competent participants will include opportunities to discuss, to assume a lead role, to work with others and to engage in authentic activities – i.e. activities that are valued by the community of learners both within and outside the school. If one is able to intervene in the learning process at the most opportune time to help learners interpret their experiences and to verbalize their thinking, then opportunities for learning are maximized. Such 'coaching' (Taylor *et al.* 2000) is about being responsive to the learner's thinking and utterances, not just about the task in hand but also about the learner and their interpretation of the task. Wood (1988: 80–1) calls this 'contingent teaching' and his description of the teacher as an enabler and facilitator of learning is worth quoting at some length:

> Contingent teaching helps children to construct local expertise – expertise connected with that particular task or group of tasks – by focusing their attention on relevant and timely aspects of the task, and by highlighting things they need to take account of ... We have used the metaphor of 'scaffolding' to describe this aspect of the teaching process. Built well such scaffolds help children to learn how to achieve heights that they cannot scale alone ... Contingent teaching, as defined here, involves pacing the amount of help children are given on the basis of their moment-to-moment understanding. If they do not understand an instruction, the teacher steps back and gives the child more room for initiative.

Contingent teaching is about attending to the learning processes, the how of learning, what learners are doing together and thinking in the course of completing a task. It is not merely attending to the product of learning in the form of the completed task. Helping children to understand what it is they are doing that causes their success or failure is the aim of this kind of teaching. If they know what to do to improve they can then 'close the gap' between what they can do or know and what they need to do or need to know. In other words, it is better to focus on causes of success and failure than to praise performance on the basis of the final product or completed task.

## Feedback to learners

This raises an interesting issue about giving feedback to pupils. If it is so important to help children understand their own learning in this way, what messages about learning are teachers conveying to pupils if they only praise them for getting work done or if they only reward their performance with stars and other extrinsic rewards? If you only praise the performance or offer extrinsic rewards, children quickly learn that it is the performance or the task itself that matters, not the learning that the task demonstrated or facilitated (Black & Wiliam, 1998a). The emphasis is placed on performance goals rather than the more important learning goals. The learner will probably be left not knowing how to 'close the gap' between what they know and, as yet, do not know and/or they will be left not knowing what learning goal to strive for next. You also run the risk of denying the learner the pleasure of taking control of their own learning, of recognizing real achievements and of setting challenging learning goals for themselves (with your assistance).

A fascinating study on children's explanations for other children's learning difficulties vividly highlights the need for a style of teaching that attends to the processes of learning and particularly for a style of teaching that helps children understand why they may be failing or succeeding in their efforts to learn. O'Sullivan and Joy (1994) investigated children's understanding of learning problems, specifically their beliefs about the causes of reading problems and how they might be overcome. They presented the children, who varied in age, with descriptions of fictitious children with reading problems. The children's task was to determine the cause of the fictitious children's reading problems and to recommend solutions. The children attributed effort, but not competence, a major role in the cause and remediation of reading problems. The children in the study persisted in saying that the (fictitious) children, who were presented as hard-working and good at obeying their teachers, should simply 'try harder'. This would lead you to conclude that children believe learning is heavily influenced by effort and, as such, very much within the control of the individual.

While this might be desirable, it is made problematic by the finding that children's beliefs about the role of effort in determining learning problems are naive – for example, they implicated insufficient effort as the cause of the problem even for children who were described as hard workers. The researchers in this study say that, because teachers rarely make explicit the processes involved in learning, emphasizing instead the influence of time and practice, they may be contributing to children's somewhat naive beliefs about the role of effort in correcting learning problems.

The pedagogical implications of this are that teachers need to attend to the processes of learning – i.e. what is causing the success and failure – and perhaps focus less on the effort expended. We return to the theme of feedback many times in the following chapters.

## Metacognition

One of the concepts which has derived from constructivist perspectives on learning is metacognition (Garner 1987; Wray 1994). We believe it is relevant to a sociocultural view of learning since its development, like any learning, cannot be separated from context or from other people in the learning community. Metacognition refers to the ability of the learner to reflect on and evaluate the thinking process itself; it refers to thinking about thinking. Metacognitive strategies would include self-awareness processes like questioning oneself to clarify the purpose of a task, searching for the main ideas and seeking connections with what one already knows or with what conflicts with what one already knows. Such processes tend to maximize the learner's control over their learning.

The learner can be helped to develop metacognitive knowledge and strategies if the teacher is prepared to spend time on the processes involved in learning and studying, and specifically to devote time to making 'strategy thinking' public. One way of doing this is for the teacher to try and make explicit the cognitive and metacognitive processes by thinking out loud while modelling a task. In other words, you need to say aloud what thinking strategies you are using as you complete a task. For example, if the task involves, say, searching for information in a non-fiction text, you might model this task yourself and as you do so, you verbalize what you are doing *and* you verbalize what thinking strategies you are applying. It seems just doing or demonstrating the task is insufficient, because then the strategic activity will be largely unobservable and the product, not the process, will be getting the greater emphasis. Garner's review of metacognition and reading development (1987) incorporates some interesting techniques for helping pupils develop metacognitive strategies for reading.

Examples of teaching strategies that would promote children's meta-cognition in reading are:

- activating the learner's prior knowledge through discussion;
- determining text characteristics – e.g. discussion of layout, use of pictures;
- determining a purpose for reading;
- generating questions;
- predicting and verifying predictions;
- reading ahead for clarification;
- looking for important ideas;
- recognizing when a comprehension breakdown occurs;
- trying to understand how the learner is functioning, trying to get at underlying misconceptions (e.g. using a running record or cloze procedure exercise to assess comprehension).

The research on metacognition and reading, for example, suggests that good readers know more about reading strategies than poor readers, detect errors in texts and recall more ideas. They have a wider range of strategies to call upon as text difficulty increases and use such strategies more often than poor readers – they are more metacognitively aware. Also, researchers have demonstrated that comprehension problems among unsuccessful readers with reasonably adequate decoding skills are often related to their failure to participate strategically while engaged in the reading process. Poor readers often do not realize when they do not understand. To comprehend text it seems the reader needs to engage in 'planful reflection' (e.g. 'I will try to grasp the main idea here') and in strategy evaluation to monitor cognitive progress (e.g. 'Oh, my mind was wandering, I must reread the last paragraph again').

## So what kind of assessment is in line with what we know about learning?

First we would suggest that while there is a growing acceptance on the part of educational professionals of learner-centred perspectives on assessment, this acceptance is less evident on the part of policy makers, a theme we return to in the next chapter. The traditional view of assessment as being about measurement in the form of pencil and paper tests still reigns supreme, with all that it implies for the way teachers teach.

As we have argued above, just as learning is a social process, so too assessment is a social process. The way the learner interprets the learning context is vitally important to their success in that context. Similarly the way a pupil interprets an assessment task is also vital for how they perform on that task. We can never assume to know precisely how a pupil may interpret or misrepresent to themselves the demands of an assessment task. Therefore, it behoves the teacher to try to anticipate or work out how the pupil might respond to the demands of a task.

Throughout this book we argue that assessment needs to be designed to promote the attainment of learning goals and to be woven into the act of teaching. We believe in aiming for the development of teaching approaches that have two interrelated purposes: the development of authentic learning and the generation of evidence of that learning. Evidence could be a combination of the following:

- what learners say;
- what learners do;
- what learners produce.

How do we generate evidence of authentic learning? Nuttall (1987) describes the types of task that validly assess learning as follows:

- tasks that are concrete and within the experience of the individual;
- tasks that are presented clearly;
- tasks that are perceived as relevant to the current concerns of the learner.

Such tasks, he argues, allow the pupil to demonstrate 'best performance' because they are 'elaborative', by which he means they promote extended interaction between pupil and teacher and they allow for a range of responses. The value of such tasks, in our view, lies in their ability to allow the teacher to get into the child's thinking and reasoning, to observe the child's strategies, dispositions and attitudes to learning, and to get a glimpse of the child's potential. In a phrase, they have the capacity to inform the next steps of learning. In addition, their value lies in the opportunity they have for the provision of quality feedback to the learner – an essential ingredient for helping the learner bridge the gap between what they know and what they need to know.

The use of multiple response modes allows pupils to respond in a variety of ways (e.g. making/doing, talking, writing etc.) and thus demonstrate their learning in a variety of ways. By adopting this approach, interpretations of evidence can be made on patterns among information sources, thus avoiding weighting single sources of information, like, say, in a pencil and paper test. By looking across several instances in which a child uses, say, reading, the teacher gets valuable diagnostic information about that child as a reader. The interpretation of the assessment information ought to be a collaborative activity between the teacher and the pupil since this kind of dialogue supports the learner in getting a handle on success criteria. This enables the pupil to gain more control of the learning process, to develop some of the metacognitive aspects noted above, and thus learn how to learn. The emphasis is on process, quality of understanding and self-assessment. The traditional model of assessment emphasized measurement and testing and taking snapshots of performance at single points – the aim being to measure individual capacity. The kind of assessment that really should matter, however, is assessment that *develops* that capacity (Gipps 1994a).

Assessment that enhances learning capacity would make the criteria of success explicit and this raises again the issue of feedback. In this model of assessment the allocation of grades or scores, or even the confirmation of correct answers, do not provide adequate feedback since these approaches will not help the learner identify what they must do to improve their performance. The argument deriving from Vygotsky is that teaching needs to be directed towards what the learner might do with support, what they might be able to do *next*, not what they can do now, independently. Consequently, feedback should be related to what the learner should do to produce a better piece of work. We will return to this important theme of feedback in several later chapters but for now we emphasize that in terms of the teacher's role, there are two key aspects of practice which are essential to the effective implementation of this assessment model:

- making learning intentions and assessment criteria explicit;
- providing a role for the learner in the assessment dialogue.

## Formative assessment: two types

We believe it is helpful to distinguish between two types of formative assessment, namely *planned formative assessment* and *interactive formative assessment*. Here we draw on the insights of Cowie and Bell (1999). These authors suggest that planned formative assessment is used to elicit permanent evidence of the thinking of pupils and such assessment occasions are semi-formal and may occur at the beginning and end of a topic. A specific assessment activity is set for the purpose of furnishing evidence that will be used to improve learning. They depict the process diagrammatically as shown in Figure 1.1. The purpose of the act of assessing is to improve teaching and learning. Information is elicited through the task or activity set, this information is interpreted and the teacher and/or pupil acts on this information with reference to the topic itself, with reference to the pupil's previous performance and with reference to how the learner and the teacher are proposing to take learning forward.

Interactive formative assessment, on the other hand, is described by

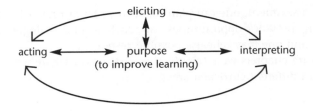

**Figure 1.1**  Planned formative assessment
*Source*: Cowie and Bell (1999: 103)

Cowie and Bell as taking place during teacher-pupil interaction. This is the kind of incidental, ongoing formative assessment that arises out of a learning activity and cannot be anticipated. It has the potential to occur at any time during interaction – whole class, small group, individual etc. As before, the purpose is to improve learning by intervening or mediating in the pupil's learning. The process is described in Figure 1.2. The process involves the teachers 'noticing', 'recognizing' and 'responding' to pupil thinking. It is more teacher- and pupil-driven than curriculum-driven. Unlike the kind of permanent information that accrues from planned formative assessment, this kind of assessment generates information or evidence that is ephemeral. The teacher notices information about learners' thinking and acting – comments, questions, non-verbal information such as how learners did the activity or how they interacted with their peers. The teacher recognizes the significance of the information. Cowie and Bell say recognizing is not the same as noticing, since it is possible to observe and note what a learner does without recognizing its significance. In interactive formative assessment the teacher tunes in to a pupil's prior subject or context knowledge or the learner's learning approach or strategy. The teacher responds or acts in relation to what is deemed to be worth noticing at the time and the teacher's response is immediate, unlike in the case of planned formative assessment where there is a longer time gap in responding. While one cannot easily plan for interactive

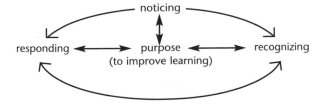

**Figure 1.2**  Interactive formative assessment
*Source*: Cowie and Bell (1999: 107)

formative assessment, one can plan for it in so far as one facilitates talk and interaction, provides opportunities for teacher-pupil dialogue and for observation, and one may rehearse possible responses.

In future chapters we return to this distinction where we exemplify assessment in different curricular areas.

## Conclusion

In this first chapter we have identified and discussed some key ideas about learning and its promotion. We have also highlighted some implications for assessment. We now consider official policy on assessment in this country and the fit between policy and theoretical perspectives.

# 2 Formative Assessment and Official Policy: Issues and Challenges

Did you know that the English invented tests?

No! But I'm not surprised.

## Introduction

In this chapter we trace the setting up and development of an official national policy on assessment. We draw attention to how this policy was informed by research from a past age, dominated by politicians and scholars who saw intelligence as a fixed commodity and regarded assessment as an exact science. As one researcher wrote, 'Public examinations were the great discovery of the nineteenth-century Englishman. Almost unknown at the beginning of the century, they rapidly became a major tool of social policy' (Roach 1971: 3).

We trace the struggles of the Task Group on Assessment and Testing (TGAT), the compromises which were made and the changes that continue to be made to the assessment system. This is shown to be a period dominated by policy makers' commitment to testing and examinations as a means of improving standards of attainment. Since the commissioning and publication of the Black and Wiliam review of formative assessment research (1998b) however, there has been a groundswell of determination to recreate a more balanced approach to assessment. This would focus on assessment that is not just used to measure pupils' progress but also to improve the quality of learning they experience.

We consider it is important to understand the context in which teachers, who are now called upon to implement formative assessment, operate. We recognize the complexities involved in this aspect of teaching and the changes of mindset that may be needed, at all levels in the education system, if the aim is to create a better balance between 'assessment of learning' and 'assessment for learning' in the primary classroom. As part of our awareness-raising we invite readers to contrast the national priority for testing with the focus of a case study, undertaken during the early years of the implementation of the National Curriculum assessment policy, and shared in Chapter 8.

## Pre-National Curriculum assessment policy and practice

Public forms of assessment, by way of examinations, have had and still continue to have greater credibility in the eyes of the general public than other forms of educational assessment. This is because of the high-profile nature of the tests and the accompanying accreditation that often open the way to higher education and/or to better forms of paid employment. A study of the research literature reveals that elementary and then primary schools have not been free from these pressures.

After the 1870 Education Act, the Endowed Schools Commission was responsible for one form of selection, that of choosing children from public elementary schools for secondary-school scholarships. This route was greatly expanded after 1907 with the creation of local authority secondary schools, and the Free Place Regulations which required grant-maintained schools to offer a quarter of their places to elementary school pupils (Sutherland 1977). Broadfoot (1996) argues that the industrialization of England in the Victorian period and the changes from a class-based society meant that new forms of social control had to be established and formal assessment techniques by way of examinations answered this purpose. Competence could be demonstrated through the successful completion of an examination and resulting certification was proof of that competence. The main purpose of the assessment instrument was to identify differences between individuals and to exaggerate the effect. To this extent the provision of an apparently fair competition, it may be argued, controls the build-up of frustration among those who fail to qualify.

A test for assessing competence was soon translated into a competitive examination. By 1936 it had become formally recognized as a selection device in which 'The purpose of the examination is the selection . . . of children fit to profit by secondary education ... The main business is to get the right children' (Sutherland 1977: 144). Intelligence testing, as part of this selection procedure, became of enormous significance in providing an acceptable means of rationing grammar school scholarship places, and after the 1944 Education Act (Raynor 1989), *all* grammar school places. These formal assessments were based on the belief in the fixed nature of aptitude and intelligence. They were associated with psychometrics and were surrounded by the scientific aura of objectivity, standardization, reliability and limited dimensions. They were also norm-referenced; in other words they yielded grades of an individual's performance in relation to their peers. They were designed by specialists to display scores on a normal distribution curve with recognized proportions gaining high, medium and low scores. But tests of this nature are more limited than might be expected and academics at the time were already beginning to question their usefulness, although the general public and teachers continued to display trust in their results (Wood 1987). The skill or attribute, which is known as the construct, is identified before the test is constructed to ensure validity. Such tests, therefore, only assess what they are designed to assess; in other words a standardized reading test score may only assess one aspect of reading skill (e.g. comprehension of simple sentences) and not the individual's ability to read in the wider sense. In order to understand the results of such a test the user of the score would need to know what had been tested. The major effect of this test on primary schools was the introduction of streaming (placing in classes in order of ability) which became common from the age of 7 upwards, in order to give 'bright' (academic) children the maximum chance of passing the eleven-plus. Because the test was high profile it also led to a narrowing of the curriculum as many elementary school teachers taught to the test (Gipps 1994a). It is worth noting that examinations such as the eleven-plus did prove a means of upward social mobility for the academically inclined children of lower-paid workers.

The wartime years from 1940–5 and the period following the war was a time of unprecedented change in schools as the school took on welfare as well as academic functions (the school meal service, medical and psychological services and pastoral systems). One consequence of this was that teachers began to see their role as extending outside the classroom; to see the child in terms of a social as well as an intellectual being. This had a profound effect on many classrooms as teaching reflected the needs of a creative rather than an adaptive being. This may be regarded as the start of a trend away from whole-class teaching towards more individualized courses of study, although it represents a general direction rather than a description of all schools at the time (The Open University 1990).

During the 1950s the concept of intelligence as fixed and inherited gradually gave way after a series of research studies showed that social class and environment influenced intelligence (Halsey and Gardener 1953; Simon

1953), although these studies did little to dispel the notion that intelligence could be tested objectively. Rather, after the Plowden Report (1967), it fuelled the need for compensatory education; for the establishment of educational priority areas where additional funding might help overcome pupils' background disadvantages. Events came to a head when a National Foundation For Educational Research (NFER) study in 1957 (Vernon 1957) showed that 122 pupils out of every thousand had been wrongly assessed in the eleven-plus. A growing political unease with this form of selection led eventually to the commitment to comprehensive schools, in Government Circular 10/65 of 1965, where the intention was that all pupils would have an equal chance of attaining their potential (Broadfoot 1996). The predominant mode of teaching, however, was still the transmission model (behaviourism) with assessment related to norm referencing. This major period of change failed to consider the relationship between teaching, assessment and individual learning. Perhaps more thought should have been given to considering the relationship between learning and assessment in order to improve individual performance, rather than to teaching an identified body of knowledge followed by grading individuals in relation to peer achievements. This was still the predominant mode of learning and assessment at the time.

Just prior to the implementation of the National Curriculum, Wood (1987) was drawing attention to researchers such as Glaser (Glaser and Strauss 1967) who had begun to explore criterion rather than norm referenced assessment for testing purposes. Here pupils are reported against specific standards, grades or criteria rather than those determined by averages or norms. Influenced by constructivism (Piaget 1972; Vygotsky 1987), researchers were looking for a 'best fit' rather than a 'typical performance', and this relates well to Vygotsky's (1987: 212) 'zone of proximal development' (the learning zone in which the pupil is perceived to be operating). Within this 'zone' the assessment tester and pupil collaborate to produce the best performance rather than withholding such help to produce a typical performance. This kind of assessment is also called ipsative or self-referenced assessment. Records of achievement, profiling and course work components in General Certificate of Secondary Education (GCSE) examinations can be seen as outcomes of this movement (Broadfoot 1996). At last assessment as a tool for learning, as opposed to placing pupils in rank order, seemed a possibility.

## The emergence of the national assessment policy

The picture emerging from the 1965 to 1987 period is of significant changes in secondary assessment practices in line with curriculum changes, as for example the Certificate of Secondary Education (CSE) and the General Certificate of Secondary Education (GCSE) examinations, with less well developed changes in the primary phase. The survey on testing practice and the use of assessment carried out at this time by Gipps and Goldstein (1983) confirm that English primary teachers, prior to the 1988 Education Reform Act, were unsophisticated in their approach to assessment. Testing was taking place with record keeping and the marking of work making up teachers' repertoire for evaluating pupil performance. There was little understanding, however, of reliability, validity and accuracy in test construction, administration or marking. Gipps and Goldstein's survey indicates that teachers were acting as technicians in applying standardized tests, but were not using data creatively to identify trends or to provide remedial help for their pupils. Shipman (1983) confirmed that much classroom assessment was intuitive and not referenced to anything. Wood (1987) also raised a concern that teachers did not relate test and examination results to their teaching and pointed out that teachers still saw these results in terms of the fixed attributes (intelligence) of the pupil. More worrying was the finding that teachers had great difficulty talking meaningfully about assessment (Gipps and Goldstein 1983).

Thomas (1990: 111) makes a very pertinent comment as he describes the situation at that time: 'assessment is relatively detailed, informal and undertaken in the course of the day's work' and 'assessment of this kind is probably one of the most difficult parts of a teacher's job, but far less time is given to it in initial training and in-service training than is given to child development in general terms'.

The emphasis on individualism and normalized stages of child development influenced by the work of Piaget (1972) did lead to major changes in the way many teachers operated in their classrooms. In the late 1970s, however, deteriorating economic circumstances became linked with concern over the perceived lowering standards in schools and a condemnation of so-called 'progressive' forms of teaching influenced by constructivism occurred. In subsequent years too few resources were allocated to the development of teacher assessment in the race to improve standards (Black and Wiliam 1998b), with teacher assessment gradually becoming less important when compared with externally set tests. In 1976 concern was expressed about educational standards in English schools by the Labour Prime Minister James Callaghan in his speech delivered at Ruskin College (Callaghan 1987). By 1988, when the Tory Party published the Education Reform Act, not only had the government changed but so had the emphasis on assessment. Whereas the 1977 Green Paper rejected regular testing of all in basic skills, the 1985 White Paper, *Better Schools* (DES 1985) issued by Sir Keith Joseph (Raynor 1989) contained the first suggestions that some form of national testing should be introduced into the final year of the primary school. This was to echo the national criteria that had been introduced for the new GCSE. These criteria were the first direct intervention by a government in the control of the curriculum and examinations in this country; previously the independent examination boards had determined examination syllabi. Arguably this set back the cause for the development of teacher assessment, although even at that stage if the education minister Kenneth Baker had listened to his advisers this need not have been the case (Black 1997). Possibly if as much consideration had been given to teacher training in assessment procedures to promote learning, teachers would have been less vulnerable to criticism, and we believe researchers such as Lawlor (1989) would have had less influence at government level in advocating a return to more traditional teaching methods.

## The TGAT report

The assessment and testing task group set up by Baker in 1987 was part of the Conservative government's plan to implement some form of national curriculum and assessment proposal in their 1987 election manifesto. All three main parties had similar goals (Black 1997). Black and his colleagues (who formed the group) were committed to enhancing the teacher's role in assessment but were tempered by caution because they were aware of the situation in schools. A private report by Her Majesty's Inspectorate of Schools (HMI) described teachers' assessment practice at the time as 'a plethora of assessment, implemented in a generally uncoordinated way and ineffective in providing for pupils, teachers and parents and the outside world a clear and full picture of pupils' progress, attainment or potential' (Black 1997: 26). The group did not believe that external testing alone provided a satisfactory answer to raising standards, but while recognizing that formative assessment held the key to improving learning and standards, admitted that teachers needed support from experts in raising the quality of teacher assessments.

The setting up of this group provided a hopeful sign that teacher assessment for the purpose of improving pupil learning was being given greater consideration. It is worth remembering that it was the TGAT report that put the terms 'formative, diagnostic, summative and evaluative' into common circulation and defined them. The distinction between formative and summative was as follows: 'Formative, so that the positive achievements of a pupil may be recognised and discussed and the appropriate next steps may be planned' and 'summative, for the recording of the overall achievement of a pupil in a systematic way' (DES 1988, para. 23). An important aspect of the TGAT report was that teachers' assessments would be central to the new system. The plan was that teachers should continue assessing pupils' performance using their own informal methods and this information would be used to support teaching. At the end of each key stage these teacher assessments would be summed up and used as part of the reporting system. The TGAT was the first report to make a significant difference to both professional and public thinking in relation to ongoing assessment and the teacher's role in this. In other words, it gave it a new form of credibility.

The first revolutionary feature of the report was the introduction of ten levels identified by a series of assessment criteria or statements of attainment which were to form a broadly criterion-referenced assessment system. Another innovation was the emphasis on criterion referencing (performance against identified task features), as opposed to the more usual norm referencing (comparison with peer performance on tasks). A further innovation linked teachers' assessment and test results and offered a platform for group moderation of both sets of results.

This was seen as a significant move forward in promoting the importance of formative teacher assessment. However, the TGAT report confused policy and practice by suggesting that formative teacher assessment could be aggregated in a structured way to provide an overall picture of the pupil (DES 1988, para. 25), thus leading to a summative evaluation of attainment. The message that formative and summative assessment is easily related in this way was further confused by concern for standardization 'in order to ensure comparability between pupils' (DES 1988, para. 44). This factor is relevant in relation to summative assessment, which may be used to make comparisons between pupils or for whole-class or whole-school profiles. When set alongside the view that summative assessment could be made from simple aggregations of formative assessments however, it led to the inevitable conclusion that formative assessment should be standardized. This apparently simplistic view brought a fundamental confusion in the minds of teachers which it is claimed has had a detrimental effect not only on formative but also on summative assessment (Harlen and James 1997).

The thrust of the TGAT assessment proposals was revolutionary and (with the luxury of hindsight) ahead of the time, but their value for improving learning (and given time, standards of attainment) was not appreciated by policy makers and as a result the potential was not realized. In other words, while (at the time) Black and his committee saw both formative and summative assessment as an integrated part of the new assessment system, central government ministers like Baker regarded assessment more simplistically as a means of enforcing the National Curriculum (Gipps *et al.* 1995). As Black (1997) writes, once the report was in the politicians' hands there proved no time for piloting strategies and decisions were made arbitrarily by ministers with minimal or no consultation. What TGAT suggested in 1988 was that:

> an individual subject should report a small number [preferably no more than four and never more than six] profile components reflecting a variety of knowledge, skills and understanding to which the subjects give rise ... Each profile component ought to be assessed separately and separately moderated.
>
> (DES 1988, paras 35–6)

These ideas for profile components were never implemented and broadly conceived attainment targets replaced the specific types of learning which each subject might require. Opportunities for formative assessment to improve pupil learning and progress could be said to have been sacrificed in favour of the summative assessment of achievement (Calfee 1996).

Baker found the recommendations made by the TGAT committee too costly and from mid-1988 the evolution of policy and practice lay with the new School Examinations and Assessment Council (SEAC) and government ministers (Black 1997). Daugherty, as a member of SEAC throughout this period, fully documented the events (Daugherty 1995), but suffice it to say that standardized tasks and emphasis on teacher assessment gradually gave way to more cheaply administered tests. Black writes of the history of the TGAT report as a 'struggle for power between competing ideologies ... the TGAT report was an aberrant obstacle in the path of a right-wing bulldozer' (1997: 27). Researchers have proposed a conspiracy theory (Lawton 1992) maintaining that the conservatives were afraid of being subverted by left-wing ideologies (Marsland and Seaton 1993). Lawton writes, 'the dominant feature of the Tory Mind which has emerged from this study is, unsurprisingly, an exaggerated concern for traditional and past models of society' (1994: 144). Black admits in retrospect that the TGAT proposals were too hastily drawn up and presented because Baker insisted on unrealistic time limits for completing the work. He admits too that the proposals were flawed but maintains that nothing better has been put in their place. He writes that:

> an outstanding obstacle to improving the current split, between summative testing for accountability and formative assessment for planning and improving learning, is that the public generally and policy makers in particular have a very imperfect understanding of the functions and limitations of assessment and testing and of their interactions with effective learning.
>
> (Black 1997: 46)

At the time, some good formative assessment initiatives were in place. The Primary Language Record was published in 1988 and proved a good framework for the new National Curriculum assessment within English. As teachers we recall incorporating aspects of it into our own practice. Based on observation of how pupils' learn and how they develop skills, the Primary Language Record alerted teachers, like ourselves, by helping us gain understanding of what we were looking at, by identifying what was significant in our pupils' learning, as was shown by their learning behaviour. Five dimensions of learning were focused upon as significant (Barrs *et al.* 1990):

- pupils' developing confidence and independence as language users;

- pupils' growing experience of language usage;
- learning strategies which pupils develop;
- pupils' knowledge and understanding of language;
- pupil's growing capacity to think about their own language and its use.

As there was to be no reported assessment for Key Stage 2 until the summer of 1995, schools started to ensure that their record keeping and systems for internal assessment were carefully developed and many turned to the Primary Language Record as a good model for gathering such evidence. Another model that was popular in the early days of the National Curriculum was the Modbury (Modbury County Primary School 1990) tick box system which many teachers embraced as a means of becoming familiar with the statements of attainment contained in the new National Curriculum. Many became increasingly unhappy with this system, however, because it reduced teacher assessment to a series of yes/no questions and they gladly jettisoned it once the post-Dearing (1994) slimmed-down version of the National Curriculum was in place.

Generally, however, teachers' intuitive formative assessment continued (as it had done before the 1988 Reform Act) with high-profile mandatory tests becoming the norm at the end of key stages (at ages 7, 11 and 14), and eventually optional tests becoming available for use in the intervening primary years. Teacher assessment was (and is expected to be) carried out throughout the key stages with results summed up at the end of a key stage (summative) to be reported to parents alongside the test results. These results are also used to compile league tables of the results of schools and LEAs and to monitor national standards (Black and Wiliam 1998b). Some researchers have written optimistically (Gipps 1994a) that English education is ready for a change from testing back to assessment that can inform learning, but as has been argued earlier in this chapter such a golden age does not appear to have existed in this country.

## A critique of National Curriculum assessment policy and practice

The administration of national tests has proved costly not only in terms of money, 'estimated as £100,000,000 in the *Times Educational Supplement*, 7 March 1997' (James and Gipps 1998: 290), but also in terms of the high-profile nature of the tests and the effect on pupils' learning. This is because they have led to greater emphasis on the types of 'surface' or 'rote' learning which are assessed (memorization, recall of facts and the display of basic skills). Researchers express concern about 'the privileged position that these tests give to certain types of learning, which constitute only a limited selection of the types of learning that the National Curriculum is designed to promote' (James and Gipps 1998: 290). The types of learning that are not promoted by this approach are of the more creative and problem-solving variety often referred to as 'deep learning' (James and Gipps 1998: 288).

Assessments of the kinds of learning which aim to discover pupils' understanding of ideas and processes are possible in the school situation, but have never been developed as a meaningful part of the national assessment policy. Prior to the National Curriculum the Assessment and Performance Unit (APU) used extensive practical tasks to find out how far pupils understood or could apply ideas. In the early years of the National Curriculum assessment, at Key Stage 1, teachers found some of the practically based Standard Assessment Tasks (SATs) to be very informative. They were 'enjoyable and motivating for the pupils, who were mostly unaware that they were being tested' (James and Gipps 1998: 291). These forms of assessment took time to administer and were quickly abandoned in favour of more simply administered tests.

Researchers admit that it is not advisable or even desirable to always concentrate on deep learning (James and Gipps 1998: 288), but neither is it appropriate in this technological age to concentrate almost exclusively on surface or rote learning. The form of assessment used has a profound effect on the type of learning pupils' experience in their classrooms (James and Gipps 1998). The lay public are more familiar with traditional tests and distrust the results of newer forms of assessment (and in these days of public accountability their opinions are taken seriously through the ballot box). However, as Daugherty (1997) argues, it is possible to train teachers in the use of more 'authentic' (Calfee 1996: 105) forms of assessment (dialogue, records of achievement) and to moderate teachers' judgements in ways that would gain public confidence.

Since the review of formative assessment research by Black and Wiliam (1998b) the importance of getting assessment that begins inside the classroom right (see Chapters 6 and 8) seems to have been accepted by policy makers. More positive messages are now being spread by organizations such as the Qualifications and Curriculum Authority (QCA) and Ofsted. Formative assessment for learning appears, at last, to be actively promoted through teacher training and to be informing changes in, for example, foundation stage assessment practice (see Chapter 11). The question that currently worries researchers and practitioners alike is whether policy makers really understand the concept or whether they see it simply as a means of raising standards in specific and narrow areas of literacy and numeracy. This concern is fuelled by a recent report in the *Times Educational Supplement* (6 June 2003: 1). In it ministers are quoted as seeing a new Pupil Assessment Tracker as 'part of a campaign for promoting assessment for learning'. In the same article, teachers' unions express concern that this is another means of ensuring teacher accountability. Dylan Wiliam, a guru in the field of formative assessment, is quoted: 'Their computer programme is like an advanced global positioning system. It may pinpoint where a hiker is down to 5 feet rather than 50, but it still doesn't tell them where they should be going or how they should get there – which is the whole point of assessment for learning'. Only teachers in the classroom can do this. In the following chapters we explore this concept through classroom incidents in regular classrooms. We invite readers to adopt an active role in the 'assessment for learning' and 'assessment of learning' debate.

# 3 Formative Assessment: What are Teachers Doing?

## Introduction

This chapter and the one that follows are devoted to considering the formative assessment practice of two primary teachers who have taught in the primary sector since 1988. The possible effects of that practice on a sample of their pupils are observed and analysed. These teachers have experienced at first hand the full effect of the curriculum and assessment changes outlined in Chapter 2. They both work in schools that are successful when judged in terms of league tables, parental choice (both are over-subscribed) and successful Ofsted reports. At the time of this case study in 1999 the teachers were chosen for inclusion because of their known constructivist practice. In the event, one teacher's practice turned out to be more prescriptive than expected. She admitted feeling 'worn down' as a result of outside pressures. Although the other teacher retained her constructivist beliefs in her practice during the case study, her health suffered not long afterwards. The pressures being exerted on schools by outside agencies adversely affected both teachers.

Formative assessment has two strands, both of which have the intention of guiding future learning in more appropriate directions than would have been possible without the assessment. The first is to inform teacher planning by identifying strengths and weaknesses, while the second feeds directly into pupil learning. In both cases these assessments are validated by the consequences (Wiliam and Black 1996). In Chapter 1 formative assessment was further divided into planned and interactive assessment (Cowie and Bell 1999). An essential prerequisite for assessment to serve a formative function for learning is for the pupil to understand the target aimed for (Sadler 1989). It is particularly important for pupils to understand what counts as quality in their work, and to be able to monitor their own progress towards these goals.

## Context for formative assessment practice

The two primary teachers involved in this study work in different schools and at the time of the study were both delivering aspects of the National Curriculum for English. The Year 4 teacher was working within the National Literacy Strategy guidelines (DfEE 1998) but the Year 6 teacher had more freedom to pick and choose because her school regularly performed highly in league tables. Mrs Fleur, the Year 4 teacher, was also the Key Stage 2 co-ordinator while Mrs Peers, the Year 6 teacher, was also the headteacher. Both teachers therefore had considerable responsibility outside their classroom teaching.

In the case study, Mrs Fleur's classroom is located in a comparatively modern building with glass partitions to corridors. Fear of disturbing other teachers appears to be a constant worry and leads her to limit talking within her class. She uses a number of behaviourist strategies, including hand clapping and drum rolls on tables to get pupils' attention and talks about training her class. Pupils indicate readiness by raising their hands or approval of others' actions by clapping.

Mrs Fleur has a classroom assistant for one hour per day and for the rest of the time she copes alone with 32 children. She groups her pupils at tables by ability. Her classroom organization for the lessons observed is a whole-class introduction, followed by activity sessions and a plenary. She admits that in the activity sessions she finds it easier to talk to a group of pupils rather than to individuals. She said of her concerns, 'The delivery of the curriculum is I think a huge influence on our practice at the moment ... You know the pressure of getting this Literacy Hour in place'. She added that as a teaching staff 'we do much more summative assessment than we do formative although we do talk about opportunities ... we share ideas for strategies'.

Mrs Peers' classroom on the other hand is located in a Victorian building with thick walls. She has 35 pupils. She does not have Mrs Fleur's worry about classroom talk disturbing nearby teachers. Flexibility in planning her English curriculum has allowed her to recruit and train four adult helpers. They are working with groups of pupils during the period of observation, thus allowing

Mrs Peers to concentrate particularly on the needs of the higher attainers. Her classroom organization also starts with a whole-class introduction but group activities are interspersed by a number of times when groups are drawn together for reflection or sharing, rather than leaving the plenary to the end of the session.

Mrs Peers has been proactive rather than reactive in organizing her school's curriculum as well as her classroom practice:

> We have a whole-school approach to it ... each of us in turn builds on what has gone before ... the difference once we had established the scheme of work and began all working in the same way on new materials to support things meant that the children were all exposed to the same way of working and we knew what had gone before ... that really did help us.

She said of herself: 'I feel confident; I constantly look for ways to evaluate my own practice; I constantly look for ways of improving it and making it better ... being the coordinator for English and the head of the school I do feel in control' (see Burke 2000a).

## Pattern of formative assessment recorded in a Year 4 and a Year 6 classroom

Formative assessment is so much a part of teaching and so complex an area to study that a decision was made to adapt a model developed by Torrance and Pryor (1998) to describe the various elements of formative assessment observed in mainstream classroom practice. This was done in order to help form a picture of the pattern and balance of assessment activities taking place. Torrance and Pryor identified 14 categories and labelled them A to P (they did not use the letters I or O). Some of these categories are not fine grained enough for detailed analysis because they contain more than one activity or indicate a different power relationship between the participants. For example, 'G    Communicates quality criteria or negotiates them with pupils' (Torrance and Pryor 1998: 160). They do, however, act as a guide to the kind of practice being observed.

Table 3.1 is the result of the analysis of Mrs Fleur's formative assessment practice during a period of four hours of observation. A count was made for each category recorded and totals displayed as percentages. The table shows the range of formative assessment activities in descending order of frequency. A similar format is used for the Year 6 classroom in Table 3.2 (see p. 32).

Mrs Fleur appears to be largely operating within the small steps of learning during these sessions by checking on what the pupils know and

**Table 3.1**  Formative assessment practice: Year 4 classroom

| % | Category | Formative assessment activity |
|---|---|---|
| 46 | C | Teacher asks principled question (seeks to elicit what pupil knows, understands or can do); pupil responds |
| 16 | D | Teacher asks for clarification about what has been done, is being done or will be done; pupil replies |
| 8 | B | Teacher examines work done (product) |
| 8 | L | Teacher suggests or negotiates with pupil what to do next |
| 7 | N | Teacher assigns mark, grade or summary judgement on the quality of the piece of work or negotiates an agreed one with the pupil |
| 5 | K | Teacher gives and or discusses evaluative feedback on work done with respect to task and or effort and or aptitude/ability (possibly with reference to future or past achievement) |
| 3 | F | Teacher communicates task criteria (what has to be done to complete the task) or negotiates them with pupil |
| 2 | E | Teacher questions pupil about how and why specific action has been taken (meta-process and metacognitive questioning); pupil responds |
| 2 | H | Teacher critiques a particular aspect of the work or invites pupil to do so |
| 1 | A | Teacher observes pupils at work (process) |
| 1 | G | Teacher communicates quality criteria or negotiates them with pupil |
| 1 | J | Teacher supplies information, corrects or makes a counter-suggestion |
| 0 | M | Teacher suggests or negotiates with pupil what to do next time |
| 0 | P | Teacher rewards or punishes pupil, or demonstrates approval/ disapproval |
| **100** | | TOTAL |

Source: Torrance and Pryor (1998: 160)

understand. She involves pupils in order to gain understanding of how they perceive the task and whether they are clear about what they should do next. The balance of her interaction is in judging whether the curriculum has been covered and pupils have performed adequately rather than determining underlying problems and establishing short- and long-term goals with pupils. Her incidence of sharing of quality criteria is very low. She isn't punitive or given to handing out rewards in the way of stickers or stamps in these sessions, but neither does she share longer-term goals with her pupils.

When she saw these results Mrs Fleur commented that she would negotiate 'what to do next time' at the end of a piece of work. This is only a sample of her practice rather than all of it, but her comment may be interpreted to indicate a limited vision of formative assessment as a meaningful part of ongoing learning. Now we can look at the results for Mrs Peers, shown in Table 3.2.

**Table 3.2** Formative assessment practice: Year 6 classroom

| % | Category | Formative assessment activity |
|---|----------|-------------------------------|
| 19 | P | Teacher rewards or punishes pupil, or demonstrates approval/disapproval |
| 13 | A | Teacher observes pupils at work (process) |
| 11 | C | Teacher asks principled question (seeks to elicit what pupil knows, understands or can do); pupil responds |
| 11 | G | Teacher communicates quality criteria or negotiates them with pupil |
| 10 | J | Teacher supplies information, corrects or makes a counter-suggestion |
| 9 | F | Teacher communicates task criteria (what has to be done to complete the task) or negotiates them with pupil |
| 6 | K | Teacher gives and or discusses evaluative feedback on work done with respect to task and or effort and or aptitude/ability (possibly with reference to future or past achievement) |
| 6 | L | Teacher suggests or negotiates with pupil what to do next |
| 5 | D | Teacher asks for clarification about what has been done, is being done or will be done; pupil replies |
| 3 | B | Teacher examines work done (product) |
| 3 | E | Teacher questions pupil about how and why specific action has been taken (meta-process and metacognitive questioning); pupil responds |
| 3 | M | Teacher suggests or negotiates with pupil what to do next time |
| 1 | H | Teacher critiques a particular aspect of the work or invites pupil to do so |
| 0 | N | Teacher assigns mark, grade or summary judgement on the quality of the piece of work or negotiates an agreed one with the pupil |
| **100** | | TOTAL |

*Source*: Torrance and Pryor (1998: 160)

Mrs Peers uses a lot of praise and encouragement in these sessions. She observes pupils closely by standing outside a group and listening to pupils talking to other adult helpers. She asks questions both of her target group of higher attainers as well as other pupils in the room. She is very active in supplying information, giving advice and discussing issues with pupils. She shares quality criteria with pupils. She gives no grades to work in progress or homework seen during the period of observation. Mrs Peers' practice does include reference to what will happen next time but metacognitive questioning is low. She is primarily concerned with what her pupils know and can do, but nevertheless her practice appears to represent a more balanced range of formative assessment activities than Mrs Fleur's does.

## Year 4 formative assessment incident

Year 4 pupils have been writing animal haikus. Mrs Fleur has selected one pupil's work (Tina) because she recognizes that there is room for improvement. Mrs Fleur uses the poem with the intention of involving all pupils in peer assessment. She asks Tina's permission before doing this and handles the situation sensitively as she introduces the session.

*Mrs Fleur*: This is what Tina is very kindly going to share with us [pointing at white board]. It's a great thing when someone offers their work to ... because they're doing it in best faith that we are going to try and help ... so we don't want to seem ... we are going to be positively ... criticize it in a positive way if you like ... in that we're going to make helpful suggestions ... We're not going to look at it and think that's a load of rubbish ... ha ha I could have done better ... That isn't helpful is it? It's not helpful because you're saying that person's work isn't very good and it's not helpful because you are not telling them ways they could make it better ... And it does take courage for someone to hand over a piece of work for ... for a whole load of other people ... to then say we can improve on this ... we can make this a much more vivid picture or whatever ... so this is what Tina's got ... she started with her brainstorm.

**Tina's animal haiku**
Bunnies chomping grass
Willows by their tiny holes
Little and fluffy

*Mrs Fleur*: Now you can read it ... read it in your head ... Mark you are the only person who is brave enough at the moment so what did you want to say?
*Mark [higher attainer]*: About the words, it follows the pattern five syllables ... seven syllables and then five.
*Mrs Fleur*: Good, so it works ... five syllables, seven syllables and then five ... so technically it works ... it's got three lines ... five syllables ... seven syllables and then five ... does it rhyme?
*Mrs Fleur/pupils*: No.
*Mrs Fleur*: Does it give you a vivid, clear picture in your head?
*Pupils*: Yes.
*Mrs Fleur*: Do you think you could help Tina to sharpen that image? James, do you think you could sharpen that image? David, could you suggest a way we could sharpen up this image? James pay attention ... Lee?
*Lee*: I don't think chomping is a very good word.

*Mrs Fleur*: You don't think chomping is a good word ... what would you replace it with? What kind of thing when you think of chomping ... what kind of action?

*Charles*: Big.

*Mrs Fleur*: Yes Charles, quite a big action ... do rabbits chomp?

*Pupils*: No.

*Mrs Fleur*: So what would you replace it with?

*Joan*: nibble.

*Mrs Fleur*: Rabbits nibble ... nibbling it ... would be nibbling ... does that still work?

*Pupils*: No, no.

*Mrs Fleur*: Bunnies nibbling ... nibbling grass.

*Pupils*: Bun-nies nib-bling.

*Mrs Fleur*: Now can we look at the next ... shhh ... could we look at the next lines please ... bun-nies ni-bbling ... grass ... wil-lows by their tiny holes ... li-ttle ... and fluffy ... whose tiny holes are...

*Pupils*: Bunnies.

*Mrs Fleur*: So?

*Samantha [higher attainer]*: Well I've got a picture of the bunnies by their holes OK but what is little and fluffy? Is it the willows? Or the bunnies? Or the holes?

*Mrs Fleur*: It's a little bit ... the image is a bit confusing ... are the willows by their tiny holes? By the rabbits' tiny holes ... what are little and fluffy? So what are these holes anyway?

*Alex*: Rabbits ... rabbits' holes.

*Mrs Fleur*: And why are they there?

*John*: For them to sleep.

*Sally*: They live there.

*Mrs Fleur*: So that's where they live ... so what word might be better?

*Pupils*: Holes.

*Mrs Fleur*: Is it? Can we ask Tina? Tina is it your ... When you wrote your haiku was your intention to describe the rabbits or the area where the rabbits lived?

*Tina*: I don't know really.

*Mrs Fleur*: If you look over your ... what does a haiku have to have? One clear picture doesn't it? So it's nibbling grass and then you've got the willows by their tiny holes and then rabbits little and fluffy ... so the first line is about rabbits isn't it? The third line is about rabbits but the second line is a bit woolly really isn't it? It's more about where the rabbits live ... the rabbits' environment isn't it?

*Jonathan*: There is something strange ... because Tina's written willows by their tiny holes little and fluffy because that sounds as though the holes are little and ...

*Pupils*: Yes.

## Reflection on Year 4 teacher's practice

In this extract, from a much longer incident, Mrs Fleur may have the intention to be formative, but she also has a poetry unit of the National Literacy Strategy (NLS) to deliver. She had identified a gap in one of her pupil's work (Wiliam 1998: 1) and with the pupil's permission had hoped to use it to stimulate interest and to inform understanding in others before moving them on to composing their final haikus.

Viewed at a distance from the busy world of the classroom, a whole-class session with such a wide range of attainment may not be the most effective way of conducting formative assessment, with higher attainers like Mark and Samantha operating on a different level to Jonathan, Tina and others. However, the teacher is under pressure to teach two forms of poetry in a period of two weeks and this may have influenced her decision to work in this way. This may be seen as an example of outside pressures getting in the way of learning. It would appear, after studying this transcript, that rather than helping the pupils to regulate their own learning Mrs Fleur has compromised and has settled for regulating the ongoing activity so that the majority of her pupils produce a successful haiku. Tina's motivation to continue has also been risked with reassurance needed after the session that she didn't have to write the haiku which the class had agreed (Dweck 1989). Researchers draw attention to two opposing kinds of assessment: 'assessment while teaching' (Torrance and Pryor 1998: 14) and 'dynamic assessment'. Whereas the latter fully involves pupils, the former 'subordinates assessment to instruction and particularly to the periodic reinforcement of learning irrespective of whether pupils require such reinforcement' (Brown and Ferrara 1985: 80–7).

## Year 6 assessment incident

Mrs Peers is working with a higher attaining group of pupils. This assessment incident, based on a homework exercise, grew out of a discussion where pupils, in groups, had been creating dialogue for the forthcoming school production of *Babushka*. The characters concerned in the story are those who control the activity of the star and also act as commentators on the plot. The teacher has turned the dialogue, produced by one group, into a worksheet and asked them for homework to punctuate it as well as add details which will make the writing more interesting for the reader. Mrs Peers has already read the homework. Each pupil takes turns to read their work aloud while others in the group evaluate it using the quality criteria already shared with them by their teacher.

*Carrie [reads aloud]*: Who's got the map asked Starlin searching high and low . . . what map asked Starlin feeling confused . . . you're not saying you've forgot the map said Starlin disbelievingly . . . what map asked Starboo about to burst with impatience . . . the map . . . the map of the journey explained Starnee trying to get the message across . . . oh that map, it's here in my pocket said Starnee receiving the message . . . unfortunately the map didn't look much like a map any more as it was covered in sticky sweet wrappers, bits of fluff and rubbish . . . that was a close one I nearly had a heart attack said Starnee looking rather faint . . . let's get moving said Starnee beginning to get fed up with Starboo . . . open the map said Starnee explaining to Starboo how to use the map . . . which way's up asked Starboo rotating the map as if it was a steering wheel . . . right what have we got to do now asked Starnee . . . we've got to go to the village . . . what village asked Starboo not concentrating on the discussion . . . the village . . . don't you ever listen replied Staress about to explode with frustration . . . what do we have to do there asked Starboo densely . . . the light has to appear in the village answered Starnee knowledgeably . . . why asked Starboo still not with it . . . because that's what happens in the story explained Starnee slowly . . . the kings have got to get to the village to meet Babushka answered Staress to Starboo as if he were a four year old . . . oh yes I remember now said Starboo as the story came back to his mind.

*Mrs Peers*: Can we just think about what we've heard . . . can we think about the wide range of criteria . . . that we've got at the back of our books . . . because what we are doing is thinking analytically . . . to think about it . . . to pull it apart and all the component parts that have gone into making it . . . OK looking at Carrie's has she got some setting? . . . she wasn't asked to have that but has she . . . [to Carrie] Do you think you have?

*Joe*: She has when she says they're going to the village.

*Carrie*: But everyone's got that.

*Mrs Peers*: Uh huh . . . has she described anything at all?

*Ellen*: Yes.

*Mrs Peers*: Yes OK she has given us description . . . mentioned the location of the map which is a kind of setting in terms of place . . . but it does give us a description of an object or whatever and she's woven that into the dialogue . . . let's have another little look at our checklist. What other things has she got in there . . . can you justify feelings?

*Ellen*: Yes.

*Lucy*: She's got thoughts hasn't she?

*Grace*: What she's thinking.

*Mrs Peers*: OK.

*Joe*: She's got thoughts hasn't she?

*Carrie*: No I don't think so.

*Mrs Peers*: Thoughts.

*Carrie*: I've got somewhere a feeling . . . they're thoughts.

*Mrs Peers*: Mm . . . mmm . . . feeling confused . . . thoughts.

*Rachel*: A description of one . . . she's got a description of the map.

*Mrs Peers*: Yes . . . I don't know that she's got thoughts . . . she's got a lot of feelings though . . . what sort of feelings though . . . what sort of feelings has she managed to get there?

*Len*: Feeling confused.

*Mrs Peers*: Feeling confused but there are others as well.

*Hayley*: All the others were really frustrated.

*Mrs Peers*: Yep OK . . . and she's done that through how they've said it . . . good . . . she's got some nice action . . . which way's up . . . asked Starboo rotating the map as if it was a steering wheel . . . a nice bit of action isn't it? . . . and nicely described . . . on a minor point but possibly important what comes after up? . . . if you say which way's up . . .

*Len*: Question mark.

*Carrie*: Oh yes.

*Mrs Peers*: Question mark . . . key words some of those . . . OK now keep focused on those criteria. The particular ones from last week but also some of the others that we are going to try and make sure that we incorporate into our writing. Now while we're listening to Hayley . . . well done Carrie . . . you've got a lot of those . . . great . . .

## Reflection on Year 6 teacher's practice

Mrs Peers in the above incident is in charge and would appear to be operating simultaneously for both the group and individual within their zones of proximal development (Vygotsky 1987: 212). She recognizes the importance of sharing quality criteria with her learners (Frederiksen and White 1997) in order that they will understand what she values in their work and the importance of encouraging her pupils to peer assess using these criteria. She says she uses SAT criteria for this purpose and this is not problematical so long as her pupils understand the reason why this is being done and don't simply think of it in terms of test preparation. This concern is raised because these pupils revealed the important place external tests have in their minds. It is very difficult, after all, to capture meaning precisely in criteria, for in any particular usage a criterion is interpreted with respect to a target population and this interpretation relies on the exercise of judgement that is beyond the criterion itself. It is therefore a fundamental error to imagine that words will be interpreted by the pupils in the same way as teachers interpret them. This is why it is so important for teachers to have appropriate information about pupils' understanding so that they can use that information in order to focus on what the pupil needs to do to improve, rather than on the pupils' self-esteem. Like Mrs Fleur, Mrs Peers does use probes in the form of questions to elicit information, but as was seen in this assessment episode questions can close down classroom discourse. Unlike Mrs Fleur she doesn't use this practice almost exclusively, but also uses probes in the form of statements, and as Dillon (1985) found these are often more productive.

## Conclusion

Although both teachers are effective practitioners, there is a clear difference in their mindsets as well as in the contexts in which they work, which affects their formative assessment practice.

Mrs Fleur exercised 'power over' her pupils. This occurred in her class management procedures as well as in the high percentage of principled questions asked. Assessment is something that is done *to* pupils in this classroom rather than done *with* them, although as Torrance and Pryor (1998) suggested this may not be consciously done. Mrs Peers' formative assessment practice, on the other hand, indicates a better balance between the assessment opportunities offered with both the short- and longer-term goals shared with her pupils. She does not appear to ask many metacognitive questions (thinking about thinking) and this may be something to consider when other aspects of her practice are analysed in Chapter 4. Her classroom management is flexible and opportunistic in using voluntary help supported by training to ensure even delivery across groups.

In both the Year 4 and Year 6 assessment incidents it may be argued that the intention is formative. Whether it does close the 'gap' in learning (Wiliam 1998: 1), however, would depend on a host of personal, contextual and structural factors. One particularly important factor is the source of motivation of the pupils. Deci and Ryan (1994) refer to 'extrinsic' *and* 'intrinsic' motivation. In other words, are the pupils controlled by external considerations such as performing well on tests or internally generated goals such as learning from mistakes? Mrs Peers clearly considers how she can involve her pupils in assessment but where she often fails is in making her more implicit strategies explicit enough for her pupils to access and use them for themselves. When she read the transcripts Mrs Peers agreed that this was a trait which she recognized in herself and she could be guilty of failing to explain the strategies which she used so that her pupils could understand not only what but why she was doing something with them.

Surprisingly neither teacher keeps records of individual errors as they occur in pupil's learning, with Mrs Peers' response reflecting both teachers' practice: 'It tends to be largely in my head' or occasionally 'in a pupil's writing book' (7 January 1999). Large class sizes may account for this, but not completely. This is a missed opportunity for teachers to gather data that could be diagnostic for individual pupils. In neither classroom were classroom assistants or trained helpers used in this capacity.

# 4    Feedback, Power and the Roles of Teachers and Learners in Formative Assessment

## Introduction

In this chapter the feedback practices of the two primary teachers referred to in the previous chapter are considered within the context of the delivery of the NLS. The effect of teachers exercising 'power over' pupils as opposed to sharing 'power with' them is examined in terms of motivation theory (Dweck 1989). The pupils' perceptions of themselves as learners are focused upon through classroom incidents as well as through interviewing pupils. Black and Wiliam (1998b) report that for feedback to be effective it must be focused on what the individual pupil needs to do to improve (task-involving) rather than focusing attention onto the learner and their self-esteem (ego-involving).

## Teachers' perceptions of feedback practice

The Year 4 teacher, Mrs Fleur, said of her feedback to children, 'It might be done in a plenary . . . as the children are working I would go and sit and talk through their writing and I would make suggestions to them . . . when I mark work . . . your next step . . . setting them something they can aim for' (Burke 2000a: 115). Of her pupils' feedback to her on her written comments she indicated that this is minimal and put it down to 'I don't think I've got them well enough trained yet . . . they do read my comments but to actually put the two things together when it's a week since they wrote it . . . they possibly can't remember' (Burke 2000a: 115). This is in keeping with findings reported by Elsout-Mohr (1994) where similar resistance to taking action over mistakes was recorded.

Mrs Peers, the Year 6 teacher, said of feedback:

> I give feedback in many ways all through the lesson because if I am doing [a] question and answer session ... chalk and talk it's always interactive ... that role model informs the rest of the children ... what I'm expecting, why that particular response is appreciated ... I also give feedback as I go round checking ... that's a good example well done or even just you're working hard or great...
>
> (Burke 2000a: 126–7)

As highlighted in Chapter 1, language is the primary tool that helps us to shape meaning. Classroom talk, however, as a vehicle for shaping learning has a very specific form that is rarely encountered in social speech: that of the three-part sequence of initiation, response and feedback (IRF). The teacher opens the discourse (initiation), the pupils reply (response) and the teacher evaluates the response (feedback). This form of utterance is seen by researchers as a problem area when trying to involve pupils more directly in formative assessment (Sinclair and Coulthard 1975; Torrance and Pryor 1998). This is because pupils expect their ideas to be evaluated and this can lead them to avoid taking risks.

Tables 4.1, 4.2, 4.3 and 4.4 show separately the pattern of talk for teachers and pupils in the two classrooms, recorded during the period of observation, analysed under the headings initiation, response and feedback and expressed as percentages (Sinclair and Coulthard 1975).

## Year 4 frequency of teacher and pupil talk patterns

When considering the results shown in Table 4.1 it is clear that the teacher controls the opening and closing moves with very little teacher activity in the response mode. This indicates that a transmission mode of teaching is in operation (Scribner and Cole 1973) with Mrs Fleur having a lot of *power over*

**Table 4.1** Teacher talk (%)

| Initiation | Response | Feedback | Total |
|------------|----------|----------|-------|
| 57 | 3 | 40 | 100 |

**Table 4.2** Pupils' talk (%)

| Initiation | Response | Feedback | Total |
| --- | --- | --- | --- |
| 13.5 | 85 | 1.5 | 100 |

her pupils in verbal interaction (Kreisberg 1992: 175). When the pupils' results are considered (Table 4.2) they are found to be largely operating in the response mode with their feedback to the teacher significantly low. These figures on their own have limited meaning but do raise awareness of the possibility of limited pupil verbal involvement, beyond the response mode, in this classroom.

## Year 6 frequency of teacher and pupil talk patterns

In Table 4.3 we can see that the teacher controls the opening and closing moves in classroom oral interaction but she also responds more frequently to her pupils than was found in the Year 4 classroom. The pupils in Year 6 (Table 4.4) are largely in the response mode, like their Year 4 counterparts, but their feedback to the teacher matches her response to them, giving a better balance overall.

**Table 4.3** Teacher talk (%)

| Initiation | Response | Feedback | Total |
| --- | --- | --- | --- |
| 49 | 12 | 39 | 100 |

**Table 4.4** Pupils' talk (%)

| Initiation | Response | Feedback | Total |
| --- | --- | --- | --- |
| 26 | 62 | 12 | 100 |

## Year 4 and year 6 teachers' feedback: perception and practice

In Tables 4.5 and 4.6 both teachers' feedback practices are analysed using the Tunstall and Gipps' model (1996). Here four main categories are considered: social and evaluative (classroom values, positive and negative features); judgemental aspects (as in specifying attainment and improvement); and the more collaborative activities where the teacher and pupils work together to construct achievement both in the current situation as well as in the future. Recognition that there appeared to be a difference in how teachers described their practice compared with what was observed led to the presentation of the results of their perception and practice in order to consider areas of possible match/mismatch. The figures are all expressed as percentages.

The Year 4 teacher's feedback practice is largely concerned with specifying attainment and reinforcing social values within the classroom. The closest match between her perception of how she uses feedback to her pupils and her practice is in her social and evaluative feedback. Mrs Fleur's perception of the balance between the short-term goals shared with pupils and the longer-term strategies is more evenly balanced than occurred in her practice.

**Table 4.5** Year 4 teacher's perception of and actual feedback

| Category | Key | Perception (%) 3 March 1999 | Practice (%) April/May 1999 |
|---|---|---|---|
| Social | S (values) | 18 | 23 |
| Evaluative | A1 Rewarding | 2 | 0 |
| | A2 Punishing | 0 | 0 |
| | B1 Approving | 29 | 10 |
| | B2 Disapproving | 0 | 4 |
| Judgemental | C1 Specifying attainment | 14 | 32 |
| | C2 Specifying improvement | 9 | 16 |
| Collaborative | D1 Constructing achievement | 14 | 7 |
| | D2 Constructing the way forward | 14 | 8 |
| **Total** | | 100 | 100 |

*Source*: Tunstall and Gipps (1996: 395)

The feedback practice for the Year 6 teacher (Table 4.6) appears more collaborative than transmission-orientated, with more emphasis on social values and collaborating with pupils than making judgements about them. There is a match between the teacher's perception and practice for 'specifying attainment'. Her social and evaluative feedback is considerably greater in practice than she perceived but this may be due to the activities observed. This could also account for the emphasis on 'constructing achievement' over the other categories. The school play was paramount in her mind and a possible contributory factor to this emphasis because she was hoping to fully involve the pupils in creating dialogue. Her intention and practice is to involve pupils actively in formative assessment and this is confirmed when more qualitative data is considered.

**Table 4.6**   Year 6 teacher's perception of and actual feedback

| Category | Key | Perception (%) 7 January 1999 | Practice (%) November 1999 |
|---|---|---|---|
| Social | S (values) | 12 | 22 |
| Evaluative | A1 Rewarding | 0 | 0 |
| | A2 Punishing | 4 | 7 |
| | B1 Approving | 8 | 10 |
| | B2 Disapproving | 4 | 5 |
| Judgemental | C1 Specifying attainment | 12 | 12 |
| | C2 Specifying improvement | 15 | 11 |
| Collaborative | D1 Constructing achievement | 30 | 23 |
| | D2 Constructing the way forward | 15 | 10 |
| **Total** | | **100** | **100** |

*Source*: Tunstall and Gipps (1996: 395)

Let us turn from a statistical approach to a more qualitative analysis of the two teachers' feedback practice. This will be accomplished by observing how an assessment conversation is conducted with a Year 4 boy and how an assessment focus helped Year 6 pupils to make sense of the shared text which they are reading.

## Year 4 assessment incident

The context for this episode was a lesson on writing haikus about animals (see Chapter 3). The pupils are aware of the objective, which is to write a poem composed of three lines of five, seven and five syllables and giving one clear picture. Mark, an identified gifted and talented pupil, has completed two haikus and is the first to show them to his teacher. During this interchange other pupils form a queue behind him, waiting for the teacher's attention.

*Mark*: I've written two versions [haikus].

*Mrs Fleur*: That would be a good idea because then you can select can't you?

*Mark*: Got two possibles.

*Mrs Fleur*: OK, so what have we got?

*Mark*: My first one is . . . because I'm doing a rat it is . . . a hungry rat hiding in the dark shadows waiting for its food.

*Mrs Fleur*: Oh that's lovely . . . oh that works very well.

*Mark*: A large rapid rat sprinting down the street to get to its home.

*Mrs Fleur*: Which do you feel gives you a better picture?

*Mark* [*pointing to the first one*]: That one.

*Mrs Fleur*: And why do you think that?

*Mark*: Umm, like he's waiting in the shadows . . . and when he sees some food come along or he sees some like . . . wherever he is then he just quickly jumps out and then he gets the food because he's like hiding in the shadows . . . so people . . . so anyone can't see him.

*Mrs Fleur*: I think I agree that gives a much more vivid picture . . . that one actually . . . I mean to me that one is another animal . . . it's a different animal to that . . . I'm not sure what . . . which kind of animal I would say that was . . . but the kind of sprinting down the street to get home reminds me a bit more . . .

*Mark* [*quietly*]: Cheetah.

*Mrs Fleur*: . . . Of a dog of some kind.

*Mark* [*quietly*]: Hmm, a cheetah.

*Mrs Fleur*: You know, sprinting like a greyhound.

*Mark*: Yes.

Mark has been identified by Mrs Fleur as a gifted child (literacy), and has attended a county initiative specifically for this purpose. He found this experience invigorating, particularly as he was one of the youngest pupils there and considered that he had coped well. He is perceptive and much quicker at getting his ideas onto paper than other pupils in the class (Burke 2000a: 119–24).

This was potentially a very good opportunity for fully involving Mark as an equal partner in the assessment episode and Mrs Fleur could have listened while her pupil recovered what he had done before going on to evaluate how well he had succeeded (Ross *et al.* 1993). Her evaluative feedback delivered so early in the conversation may or may not have influenced his decision, but she didn't allow for the possibility. She exercised 'power over' her pupil rather than 'power with' him (Kreisberg 1992: 175) by failing to hear him when he was thinking aloud. She did this on two occasions. There are many reasons why this can happen in a busy classroom, not least having to supervise 31 other pupils at the same time as engaging fully with Mark. Her mind might have been, for example, on the next pupil waiting in line for her attention. So how did Mark react to this feedback? In the interview following this session he showed that he had 'appropriated' (Leont'ev 1981) his teacher's imagery and abandoned his own as he said of his second haiku idea 'that one sounded like a dog'. In this incident Mrs Fleur's transmission mode of teaching appears to be getting in the way of her fully appreciating Mark's zone of proximal development (Vygotsky 1987: 212) and adjusting her feedback to 'scaffold' (Wood 1988: 80) his learning. The classic IRF feature identified originally by Sinclair and Coulthard (1975) was very active in this classroom. Mrs Fleur controlled the talk and then she evaluated the response. On the surface the child's task was to respond not to initiate. Bernstein (1996: 163) writes that 'to a very great extent the pedagogic mode is an interrogative mode where sequences of questions "pilot" the student towards a pre-determined outcome known to the teacher'.

For feedback practice to become informative for either planning or learning purposes in this classroom a mindset shift may be necessary in order for Mrs Fleur to hear what her pupil is saying and be able to 'appropriate' (Leont'ev 1981) what her pupil is thinking.

Mark reflects on his own learning and undoubtedly self-reflects and self-corrects his work. Of the haiku he said:

> I just read it through ... I didn't know how many syllables I'd got ... I just read it and realised it was right and then I just ... a few things here I changed 'cos it ... I tried to put on my second line ... hiding in the black shadows but I already had a black rat ... so I changed black to dark ... still the same number of syllables.
>
> (Burke 2000a: 149)

He is, however, wary of his teacher's expectations of him. He knows that Mrs Fleur has added expectations for his group over others in the class and admitted that he would be reluctant to tell the teacher that something was too easy for fear that 'She might set us too hard a task and then we can't do it' (Burke 2000a: 143).

## Year 6 assessment incident

Mrs Peers is working with a group of eight higher-attaining pupils. They are reading a shared text as part of the NLS. Clear learning objectives have been shared with the pupils; these are to take turns in reading the text with expression, taking account of punctuation.

> Lucy [reading from shared text]: We had picked ourselves up now and were leaning on the parpet.
>
> Mrs Peers: Ehh, let's have a little think ... a parapet it means the edge of something like a building ... or a bridge has a parapet if it has sides where you stand and lean over the parapet or ... have you been in a castle?
>
> Len and Joe: Yes kind of.
>
> Mrs Peers: And climbed up to sort of battlement heights?
>
> Len and Joe: Yes.
>
> Mrs Peers: And that edge ... that built up edge?
>
> Rachel: Like the church tower.
>
> Mrs Peers: Yes the church tower has got a parapet ... like a wall you can see over.
>
> Rachel: And it goes down and then up.
>
> Mrs Peers: Well it's there to prevent you.
>
> Lucy: From fall.
>
> Mrs Peers: Just going off the edge ... something that is built up.
>
> Lucy [continuing to read]: It was quite dark but I didn't want to go back in...

There is evidence here of Mrs Peers' familiarity with 'miscue analysis' (Goodman 1973: 93), a method we return to in Chapter 6. This concept allows teachers to make meaningful interventions in their children's learning by taking the emphasis away from errors to understanding why competent users of the language might miscue when reading texts. This is a constructivist view of knowledge as 'miscues' provide gateways into the zone of proximal development (Vygotsky 1987: 212) by enabling teachers to help pupils build on their current understandings. This approach appears to be accepted by the eight pupils involved and Lucy ends the session seemingly motivated to keep on reading. For 30 minutes the pupils take turns to read (as instructed) with expression, and their teacher highlights 'miscues' in word pronunciation, lack of close attention to punctuation etc. She is in control and everything runs smoothly. This is in keeping with her statement 'I've got to give them a structure ... a structure that they understand' (Burke 2000a: 134).

But has she done this? At no time does she share *why* she is working in this way with the group. When she leaves the group to continue alone while she supervises other groups in the room presumably she has confidence that they can work independently.

In the follow-up incident it would appear that Mrs Peers' implicit 'scaffolding' of her pupils (Bruner 1986: 129) was not absorbed by them so that they could use it when working alone. Here, Grace is reading aloud, very slowly and quietly. Len and Joe are whispering to one another while she is reading.

---

*Grace*: We started . . .
*Len*: I'm bored with this.
*Joe*: Let's read silently.
*Len*: Let's just stop please.
*Grace*: I can't go any faster.
*Joe*: It doesn't matter.
*Rachel*: OK, well you can just listen then.
*Grace*: You have to read it alone.
*Len and Joe*: Boring . . . boring . . . boring.
*Rachel*: All right, keep going.
*Grace [hesitantly]*: And then he smiled again and pulled a roll out of his giblet . . .
*Len [laughing]*: Stupid . . . giblet.
*Grace [continuing reading]*: I'm Shakespeare.
*Len and Joe scoff.*

---

Perrenoud argues that pupils have the right to hesitate, make mistakes, reflect, enter into dialogue and thus learn (1998: 88). The teacher of these pupils appeared to agree with this perception. When she was working with this group her active and constructive approach to teaching indicated that her central focus was on the process of learning rather than the outcome. Other considerations such as the dynamics of other groups working in the same room deflect her and thus limit her ability to sit back and observe the effect of her strategies on her pupils, when left to work without her. If she had been observing this group she might have had a clearer insight into her pupils' reactions to the problem which they encountered when left to work without supervision. In turn this might have enabled her to adjust her strategies to help take account of their individual reactions. This is a missed opportunity for developing formative assessment for informing planning which hopefully would in turn influence learning. In order to be good learners, however, pupils do need to develop resilience and resourcefulness, experience real-world situations and learn from uncertainty without becoming insecure and defensive. One could argue that the teacher has provided them with just such an opportunity and has the confidence to expect them to cope with the situation. Insufficient knowledge of her pupils' motivation and reactions to problems (without her presence) would seem to be a strong contributory factor. Although part of an identified higher-attaining group, Grace appears to have accepted her reading problems rather than devising strategies for overcoming them. She displays stubbornness in adapting to the criteria aimed for and 'learned helplessness' (Dweck 1986: 1040) in overcoming her problems. Her limited resilience when faced with difficulties is not compensated for by the other pupils because they do not appear to have developed the resourcefulness or ability to reflect on the problem which has arisen, and thus move Grace forward. The pupils' display the four reactions identified by Kluger and De Nisi (1996). Len wants to abandon the goal completely, Joe wants to change it, Rachel wants to carry on and Grace denies the problem exists.

When interviewed these pupils admitted reliance on their teacher to make them work for most of the time. As Len remarked, 'If she didn't [make demands on us] then we just wouldn't do anything' (9 November 1999). They also admitted that their goal for the year was 'to do well on SATs'.

Mrs Peers' strategy for identifying a weakness and constructing a meaningful way forward may need to be made more explicit to her pupils for them to undertake this role for one another. The point being made here is that the teacher in the above extract is considering both the lesson criteria and the individual pupils' needs, but she has failed to communicate her intentions sufficiently clearly in order that her pupils can do this for one another. They are insufficiently aware of the success criteria aimed for in this activity.

## Reflection on both teachers' feedback practice

Both teachers clearly dominate the talk in these classrooms. The pupils are largely in a response mode. Both teachers give a lot of evaluative and social feedback but where they differ greatly is in their sensitivity to individuals' needs when addressing cognitive issues. For a variety of organizational or personal reasons they do not always listen to their pupils, or are not always in the right place to do so. They both have secure subject knowledge and are diligent in delivering the National Curriculum. Mrs Peers seems more in touch than Mrs Fleur with social constructivist research and its application to the classroom (Vygotsky 1987), but developmental constructivist traits do emerge in Mrs Fleur's practice (Piaget 1972). Both teachers' wall displays reflect a 'training model' (Calfee 1996: 100) and outside influences also impact on pupils' understanding and help create the kind of goals pupils aim for. In early September, for example, Year 6 pupils were proclaiming that their personal goals for the year were to get good SATs results. This was before Mrs Peers had mentioned SATs to them. The reality of formative assessment and feedback practice in these two classrooms is that it is 'value laden rather than factual' (Donmoyer 1995: 5) and it appears underdeveloped for learning purposes.

Teachers currently instruct pupils either implicitly or explicitly in what to do as opposed to finding ways to work with the pupils to reach acceptable personal solutions. There is an emphasis on the importance of the product aimed for and the process engaged in is largely taken for granted. Attainment is important, but if the product is prioritized over the process, pupils may be missing out on learning from others or by making their own mistakes. A focus on curriculum delivery and summative assessment pressures has been the norm since 1988 and it is not surprising that other considerations such as the needs of individual learners have gradually been pushed to one side. Mrs Fleur appears to be using feedback to influence her pupils to conform to her perceived standards and in the incident with Mark, for whatever reason, used 'power over' her pupil (Kreisberg 1992: 175) which would be consistent with the behaviourist tendencies referred to in Chapter 3. Mrs Peers is also working for high standards but her feedback to pupils appears more enabling. She uses 'power with' her pupils as she concentrates on the text rather than the individual pupil (Kreisberg 1992: 175). This is also consistent with her constructivist tendencies highlighted in the previous chapter but, as referred to earlier, her practice is not always as constructive as she aims for or would consider desirable for her pupils as learners. The differences in the emphasis on targets for achievement *leading* to high standards as opposed to targets *directly related* to high standards may not be as clear to the pupils as it might or should be. This may result from inadequate communication at the individual, group and whole-class level. On the surface pupils appear to accept feedback from their teachers unquestioningly. As has been seen, when transcripts were analysed, appearances can be deceptive because pupils do not always act upon what the teacher might have expected them to understand. They do not always recognize feedback as helpful guidance (Tunstall and Gipps 1996).

## Conclusion

Feedback, as observed in these two classrooms, appears a less straightforward concept than other researchers report (Tanner and Jones 1994) because both teachers to a varying degree lack clarity in their intentions. They are reacting to government guidelines, which at the time also did not have clarity of intention for formative assessment practice for learning. In the *National Numeracy Strategy* document, for example, formative assessment is called 'short-term assessment' (DfEE 1999: 33). The whole tenor of the writing is that it is uncomplicated to carry out and that feedback to pupils can be given in whole-class situations. Unless teachers are knowledgeable enough to read between the lines and identify the pitfalls in these supposedly well-considered proposals, unquestioned norms can distort otherwise good practice. This is a theme we return to in Chapter 7 as we observe numeracy practice in a school catering for large numbers of pupils for whom English is not their mother tongue.

# 5  Helping Learners Understand How Their Work is Judged

## Introduction

If we accept that learners are active meaning-makers and that learning requires their willing participation and active intellectual engagement, then it
follows that teaching involves finding ways of supporting learners' meaning-
making and motivation to participate. But what does it mean in assessment
practice to recognize the active role of the learner? Here we address this
question with reference to helping learners understand how their work is
judged. In view of the fact that the learner is the ultimate user of it, we
consider how we should help learners understand and use assessment information. One key aspect of this is helping learners come to know the criteria against which their work is judged and to recognize a successful product
– a prerequisite for effective self-monitoring. The chapter then describes and
explains procedures for making explicit the standards, criteria and targets that
are too often left implicit for learners to discover on their own. Pupil self-
assessment and peer assessment are both vehicles for and outcomes of understanding the standards against which work is evaluated. The chapter
discusses the professional and practical implications of supporting these

assessment approaches. The chapter concludes by describing 'the dialogic classroom'.

## Providing a participatory role for the learner in assessment

It is clear by now that assessment is not simply about the teacher checking that information has been received by the learner. That outmoded view of assessing fits with a notion of learning and teaching that assumes skills and knowledge can be taught in isolation and then applied automatically in new contexts. It also assumes that knowledge is fixed and certain and can be unproblematically lifted and applied to new situations. We now know that learning that is not made meaningful to the learner or learning that is not tuned into prior learning and experiences is soon forgotten. On the other hand, learning that is applied in meaningful contexts, learning that is linked to previous experiences and understanding, endures because it becomes embedded in the learner's cognitive framework and becomes part of the person's identity (see Gipps 1994b).

While most teachers appreciate the role of assessment in informing the next steps of their teaching, only recently have they become more aware of the need to help learners use assessment information to improve their learning. Knowing what to do next to improve is crucial for the learner and in the past policy makers have not recognized the significance of this knowledge for learners, though it has been recognized for some time by researchers. What is clearly emerging from the research on formative assessment is that teachers are accountable first and foremost to the learner. As we argued in Chapter 2 currently there is emphasis at the level of policy on system accountability at the expense of accountability to the learner.

In their review of the evidence on formative assessment Black and Wiliam (1998a, 1998b) emphasize how the learner is the ultimate user of information from formative assessment. So what information do we make available to our learners about how they are doing? If we only give them grades or marks or 'gold stars' then we shouldn't be surprised if our pupils devote their energy to obtaining those rewards. They will seek clues as to the right answers rather than attend to the needs of their learning – they will be performance-orientated rather than learning-orientated. In such a classroom climate pupils may avoid challenging tasks and not ask questions out of a fear of failure – their energies are concentrated on performance goals, not learning goals (Dweck 1989).

Feedback would appear to be the key to a positive culture and to promoting learning goals rather than performance goals. Feedback explains what is wrong and what is good about puplis' work, and it suggests ways forward and ways of correcting it that make sense to the learners (not just to the teacher). Feedback directs teacher attention to what needs to be taught and pupil attention to what needs to be learned – it is integrated into the teaching and learning. It is characterized by attending to the learners' understandings, learning strategies and dispositions to learn, and it engages with the way learners interpret the assessment tasks set and the criteria for their success.

Feedback is important for all learners but the research evidence shows that it is especially important for low achievers. Why is this so? A salient feature of feedback is that it makes the criteria for success explicit to learners. It is probably this factor, Black (1999) notes, that accounts for the relative gains made by pupils initially classified as 'low achievers' since it is reasonable to suggest that these pupils previously suffered from lack of clear guidance regarding what counted as success rather than from any lack of ability on their part. Lower-attaining pupils often attribute their low achievement to some presumed lack of innate ability and become discouraged and unwilling to invest in further learning. Clear guidance on what counts as success is a start towards supporting the expectation that all children can learn to high levels and begins to counteract the cycle in which children attribute poor performance to lack of ability.

Black and Wiliam (1998b: 9–13) describe what good feedback looks like and what formative assessment involves:

- relevance to the particular qualities of the pupil's work;
- advice on what he or she can do to improve;
- avoidance of comparisons with other pupils;
- setting tests and homework exercises which are clear and relevant to learning aims;
- feedback on homework which gives each pupil guidance on how to improve.

Feedback also involves:

- training pupils in self-assessment; and
- opportunities for pupils to express their understanding and thus initiate the interaction whereby formative assessment aids learning.

One important way of facilitating the second aspect is through peer assessment. Self- and peer assessment empower learners to take control and assume ownership over their learning and to recognize that they themselves are ultimately responsible for their own learning. However, learners don't necessarily possess the skills for engaging in self- and peer assessment automatically and we would argue that it is the teacher's role to equip pupils with the skills and strategies for taking the next steps in their learning. One vital way of helping learners to self-evaluate and to assess their own work and that of their peers is to equip them with some sense of what counts as 'good' work. They need to develop some notion of quality and share the same notion of quality as their assessor or teacher.

## Sharing success criteria with learners

Given the significance of sharing success criteria or what counts as quality work, it is worth considering this element of formative assessment in a little more detail. All of us have standards of quality and maturity but we do not always need to articulate them. We find Sadler's conceptualization of this process especially helpful (1989, 1998). He talks about 'guild knowledge' that teachers build up and share over time as a community of knowers and judgers of pupils' work. This guild knowledge, according to Sadler, enables the teacher to make sound judgements about pupils' work. However, he notes the problem of making this knowledge explicit since guild knowledge is not always articulated but exists as 'lore'. The challenge for teachers, therefore, is to render it explicit so it becomes available to pupils. Purves (1993) observes that 'the judge must make clear the criteria' on which judgements are made, and adds that most assessors do not do this. Not to make explicit the success criteria for a task he says 'keeps the judgement subjective, it keeps the criteria up the assessor's sleeve' (p. 175).

What follows from all this is that it is necessary to involve pupils in conversations about the quality of their work and performance so they get to apply a concept of quality that is in line with that of the teacher (Sadler 1989). Sadler advocates a process of induction or apprenticeship whereby the authoritative (but not authoritarian) teacher (a 'connoisseur' who has 'insider' knowledge regarding what counts as a good performance) explicitly supports pupils in acquiring a metalanguage or a language to talk about and assess their own performances. He advises teachers to enable students 'to develop their evaluative knowledge, thereby bringing them within the guild of people who are able to determine quality using multiple criteria' (p. 135). Other assessment researchers have argued along similar lines. Frederiksen and Collins (1989) suggest that: 'The assessment system should provide a basis for developing a metacognitive awareness of what are important characteristics of good problem solving, good writing, good experimentation, good historical analysis, and so on'. Clearly such an approach addresses not only the product one is trying to achieve, but also the way of achieving it – that is, the habits of mind that contribute to successful writing, reading, problem solving etc.

The assumption underpinning these recommendations is that simply providing feedback to the learner is not enough; in itself this does not guarantee improvement. The criteria for success must be understood by pupils in their terms and not just remain in the teacher's head. For feedback to be useful, the learner must know what to do and how to do it in order to bridge that gap between what it is they can do now and what they need to be able to do. Moreover, as Shepard (2000) observes, as well as pushing pupils towards higher standards, involving pupils in dialogue about their own work in relation to success criteria builds ownership of the assessment process and offers pupils more control over their learning.

From the above one could conclude that learners have to be aware of the criteria against which their work is judged before they can be expected to engage in self-assessment and peer assessment. However, we would argue that opportunities to talk about their work together in pairs, in small groups and as a whole class support the process of coming to know and understand the relevant success criteria. Many children, especially those who are bombarded with grades, marks and gold stars, frequently do not know the basis on which their work is judged; for them classroom life can seem to consist of moving between arbitrary sequences of exercises with no overarching rationality.

As Black and Wiliam (1998b) note, when learners do come to a sense of how their work is judged they are far more effective and committed as learners. They can self-evaluate. These authors make the point again and again in their research that self-assessment is not a luxury but an essential element of effective learning. But as already noted, it is difficult to evaluate one's own or another's work if one hasn't a language to talk about it. This language or metalanguage can be developed if teaching builds in opportunities for learners to communicate their growing understanding of:

- themselves as learners;
- the quality of their work and their present state of knowledge or skill in the topic in question;
- the desired destination for their learning; and
- ways of bridging the gap between what they can do and need to do.

All of this demands much discussion and observation. It is far from simple and requires planning and thought on the part of the teacher. Yet it cannot be entirely planned in advance since classroom discussion and exploratory talk will be spontaneous, dynamic and context-dependent in line with what we know about learning itself (see Chapter 1). As is clear also from Chapter 4, we are arguing for a more participatory role for the learner in the assessment enterprise and this in turn foregrounds the learner's opportunities to talk. It asks the teacher to adopt the role of careful listener, interpreter and insightful responder. This does not mean a non-interventionist role for the teacher, however, for as Madaus (1994: 9) points out, 'the teacher is a mediator between the knower and the known, between the learner and the subject to be learned'. In this book we are advocating a more dialogic (versus monologic) classroom where power and opportunities are more equitably shared.

For now we emphasize that through discussion and classroom talk learners display and develop the state of their knowledge about each of the points noted above. They need the chance to talk about their understanding in their own way – they need to engage in what might be called exploratory talk or learning talk. Most importantly, the teacher can tune in to this exploratory talk for herein lies the opportunity to 're-orient the pupil's thinking' (Black and Wiliam 1998b: 11), to offer ideas about how to move forward in their learning, to question and challenge interpretations about the quality of existing work, to share interpretations of work done and to describe and plan learning aims. Unfortunately, too much classroom interaction is taken up by pupils trying to work out what is in the teacher's head, what the 'correct' answer is. It is not surprising that some pupils eventually learn that they are not really expected to think for themselves, that thinking is the teacher's privilege only and that success in school is merely about completing tasks. To shift from such a scenario to one where interaction is learner and learning orientated demands time, energy and thought.

The following section incorporates some classroom strategies that primary teachers might use to promote a climate of success and to equip their pupils with the skills to self-evaluate. But it recognizes that there is no recipe or blueprint that can be presented to teachers to enable them to enable their pupils to engage in self- and peer assessment – our suggestions are therefore illustrative of the principles we have outlined in this section.

## Some dilemmas of making criteria explicit: learning as acquisition or participation?

So far in this chapter we have been advocating that teachers help their learners 'understand the standard' as if the standard is something discrete and outside of them as knowers. We recognize that the standard or the criterion by which a piece of work or performance is judged is not straightforward. This is because standards or criteria are made real by their application and interpretation in different contexts. Here we find 'learning metaphors' (Sfard 1998: 6) helpful. If you subscribe to the 'acquisition metaphor' for learning then learning is treated as 'gaining possession over some commodity'. In the context of our discussion then, the criterion lives, is out there, separate from the learner. If you subscribe, as we do (see Chapter 1) to the 'participation metaphor' and see learning involving changing roles and identities within communities of shared practice, then it follows that the criterion is inseparable from the learner, the community of learners and teacher(s) and the activity on which they are engaged. In this sense we recognize that the standards or the success criteria are emergent, non-deterministic and contingent. They have to be negotiated over, they can be contested; they have to be interpreted by those who apply them.

In line with this thinking some assessment writers (e.g. Sadler 1989; Claxton 1995) argue that what constitutes 'good work' is an intuitive act, not reducible to the application of predetermined criteria since criteria are not necessarily external, explicit and predetermined but are 'fuzzy' and at least partially revealed 'as you go along'. They may also be specific to a particular task or piece of work. We share this view. Wiliam (1998) acknowledges this and abandons the term 'criteria' altogether on the grounds that criteria are 'ambiguous', and he refers instead to 'understanding the standard' through 'a shared construct of quality that exists in some well defined community of practice' (p. 9). The learners as well as the teachers need to share notions of quality. Self- and peer assessment, in our view, offer the potential of 'enculturating learners into communities of practice' (Wiliam 1998) and are potentially powerful means of explicating and sharing assessment criteria or standards and notions of quality.

Examples of helping learners to understand what counts as good work and to apply standards or success criteria could include the following:

- teacher explains learning objectives at the beginning of a lesson;
- pupils talk about externally-specified standards and write them in their own words;
- making examples of work available for children (as well as teachers) with annotations identifying the way the work meets the standards or the success criteria;
- pupils list the success criteria;
- pupils discuss samples of strong and weak performance;
- pupils study work samples and say in detail how it could be improved;
- pupils mark one another's work and discuss their conclusion;
- pupils devise questions appropriate for the assessment of their work (rather than answering other people's questions);
- pupils discuss several samples of work and decide which are great examples, which have some good points and which are very poor, gradually developing criteria as they work; and
- pupils design their own tests to assess aspects of their learning.

Self-assessment involves thinking about one's experience, attempting to understand what has happened and working out what one has learned (Munby *et al.* 1989). The ability to self-assess is part of the learning process itself. What supports the ability to assess one's own work and that of one's peers is feedback from the teacher or from peers which pushes the learner to:

- attend to learning goals;
- devise strategies for reaching those goals; and
- monitor the discrepancy between actual and desired performance.

As Sadler (1989) reminds us, feedback, however detailed, will not lead to improvement until a pupil understands both the feedback itself and how to use it in the context of their own work. The example below is taken from a setting where the teacher placed a high emphasis on her pupils' ability to regulate and monitor their own learning, where feedback and reflection were key features of pedagogy and where pupils were encouraged to participate in setting goals for their learning.

## Self-assessment in Year 1

Sue teaches Year 1 in a coastal town in south-east England. She believes children as young as 5 are able to engage in self- and peer assessment. They are able to remember and review activities, she says. They are able to differentiate the challenging from the easy, the enjoyable from the boring and the collaborative from the individual. They have views about their learning and can reflect and talk about it. Sue routinely invites her pupils to talk about:

- what they thought they had learned in the session, what they learned today, last week etc., articulating not only the *products* of learning in a conventional sense, but also their feelings that went along with that learning (e.g. how they struggled, found it difficult, exciting and sometimes boring);
- what made a particular task difficult or tedious;
- how they learned – sharing, talking, being quiet and contemplative, reading etc.;
- what made particular work they had completed good or not so good; and
- how they could improve on it another time.

Such an approach develops reflectiveness and a respect for the feelings of learning and the feelings of the learner as well as a sense of quality and success criteria. Sue's style of teaching and interaction with her pupils communicates the message that the way we learn is something that is to be talked about and shared, that how to learn is learnable, and that pupils can enhance their learning acumen. She directs her pupils towards an increasingly complex understanding of tasks and learning goals. Through self-reflection and sharing of perceptions she develops her pupils' strategic knowledge of how to go about improving. A major part of getting to be a better learner involves getting a purchase on how one's work is judged and having strategies to reach those requirements. Sue's 5-year-olds are helped to review their learning not just in terms of concrete recording of what they did or what they learned but also in terms of relevant future learning objectives.

Here it is worth noting four phases of the learning reflection process (Greenway and Crowther 1989 in Munby *et al.* 1989) which are included in Sue's approach just described:

1   The knowledge phase – remembering events from the past with initial concrete recording in terms of 'I did' statements and differentiating statements (e.g. 'I liked').
2   The analysis/understanding phase – seeking to understand why things happened in the way they did (e.g. 'I think I worked well because...').
3   The evaluation phase – making judgements about the learning situation and evaluating what has been learned and achieved (e.g. 'the map we drew of our school didn't help our visitors find our classroom because...').
4   The synthesis phase – considering ways in which what has been learned can be fitted into an overall context, and in the light of what has been learned, deciding on relevant future objectives.

What underlies Sue's stance as a teacher is her view that coming to know is constructive – a point we tried to develop in Chapter 1. This means that pupils are agents – they are actively involved in thinking, feeling and evaluating. Their ideas, feelings and experiences influence the way they interpret the tasks and the objectives set for them. Not only that, but how they interpret the tasks and the objectives is not merely an individual matter (i.e. each pupil acting individually on their environment) but the individual is acting in a setting and in a relationship to particular peers and a particular teacher, all of whom constitute a dynamic environment. Together there is some kind of shared understanding of what it means to engage and succeed in the activities set. The learning that happens is situated.

Guy Claxton (1999) highlights misconceptions about learning that some learners, regardless of age, often hold. If one believes learning has to be fast or not at all, he argues, one will not mull over something difficult, there is no point. If one believes that knowledge is fixed and certain, one will avoid ambiguity. And if one believes that all learning leads to clear comprehension, then one won't value learning that one cannot readily identify. The point we wish to emphasize here is that it is not always easy or even desirable to chase after one predetermined learning outcome or to confine oneself to one success criterion in the course of a given activity. One of the most illuminating aspects of Claxton's research is his explanation of how the *when* and *how* of learning depend on the learner's tacit cost-benefit analysis of the situation. This means that all of us are influenced by our subjective judgements of the costs and benefits of any given learning situation and these judgements are informed by our personal beliefs and values which, in turn, may be accurate or inaccurate. We may, for example, make too much of the threats, the potential loss of face, thus misrepresenting to ourselves what the task involves, and we may, therefore, revert to defensiveness or avoidance. The major point here is that different people may perceive the same learning context differently. In this sense, 'defensiveness, seen from the inside is always rational' (Claxton 1999: 332). For the teacher, the implication is that having some sense of what the child's inner world feels like is important and an approach like Sue's opens up this world.

## The dialogic classroom

One of the interesting findings emerging from research on teacher effectiveness in recent years that is relevant to our discussion here concerns how meanings are shared and understandings are developed through dialogue in classrooms. It seems that teachers whose pupils 'beat the odds' (i.e. do better than expected for their age or compared to similar pupils in other classrooms) encourage supportive, respectful and productive talk (Taylor *et al.* 2000; Allington and Johnston 2001). Such talk is not only modelled by the teachers in their interactions with pupils, but is also deliberately taught and expected, especially at the beginning of the school year. In this way pupils learn how to talk about their learning, which is important for their ability to self-assess and peer assess their work.

The creation of 'conversational communities' was found to be a key element in the success of the most effective teachers and these teachers devoted considerable energy and time to building the kind of trusting relationships and non-judgemental contexts that are needed for such conversations to happen. Through such conversations 'interactive formative assessment' occurred (see Chapter 1). The kind of talk that characterized high achievement classrooms is described as 'tentative' – we used the word 'exploratory' above. This is the kind of talk that allows other learners to articulate their developing ideas. It also allows teachers to intervene to progress a pupil's learning or to observe and gain insights into the pupil's understanding.

This kind of talk is limited or excluded in classrooms where the teacher dominates the talk and denies pupils the opportunity to express their developing understanding orally. Such classrooms can be described as 'monologic'. Bakhtin (1981: 81) distinguishes between 'monologic' and 'dialogic' discourse. When 'monologism' characterizes interaction he suggests that '*the genuine interaction of consciousness is impossible, and thus genuine dialogue is impossible as well'*. This kind of interaction provides little or no space for learners to participate actively in the construction of knowledge; they are denied the opportunity to make meaningful contributions on their terms. When interaction is dialogic, on the other hand, the balance of discourse is more symmetrical and in the classroom the teacher's voice is 'but one voice among many' (Nystrand *et al.* 2001: 6). Alexander (2000) refers to this kind of interaction as 'dialogic teaching' and 'scaffolded dialogue' and the Teaching Through Dialogue Initiative within the NLS seeks to extend the repertoire of teaching talk in classrooms. In relation to formative assessment, interaction that involves pupils in asking more questions and that involves teachers in asking more open-ended questions is needed.

What specific contexts are associated with the emergence of dialogic discourse? We suggest that the size of the group, the nature of the tasks set, the learning objectives and teacher awareness of language as a medium of learning are all relevant factors here. Our previous research (Hall 2002; Hall *et al.* in press) shows that while recitation characterizes even small-group work and is ubiquitous in whole-class teaching, the small group seems to offer greater potential for dialogic interaction than the whole class. The reasons for this are straightforwardly practical – the teacher, being less concerned about classroom management and order, is able to loosen their hold on the discursive reins and confer more freedom and agency to pupils. Second, where the set tasks are requiring pupils to construct their own knowledge, dialogue would seem to be an important means towards that construction. Third, where teachers are quite strictly bound by predetermined learning objectives and where coverage of curricular content is accorded high status, such tight planning may constrain dialogue; it may even be seen as time-wasting. Collaborative group work, where pupils are working jointly on a common task (say evaluating a piece of work) provides the maximum opportunity for learners to share, to justify their decisions, to articulate and apply success criteria to products, to develop images of possible and excellent work.

We suspect that teachers may be generally quite unaware of the power of language as a medium of learning – certainly pupils are unaware of it (Hall 1995). Teachers may be aware of the organizational and pedagogical strategies and decisions that they use and make as they teach (e.g. whether and how to group, tasks to set, the resources they need, how to differentiate etc.). But what we suspect they are far less sensitive about is the way their discourse impacts on the learning opportunities on offer. In this sense teachers probably underestimate the importance of exploratory or tentative talk in their pupils' achievement.

The kind of questioning that teachers use to promote classroom dialogue is especially important for assessment. Thoughtful answers (i.e. answers that are not merely recalling facts from memory) require time to think – 'wait time' – on the part of the teacher to allow the learner to formulate a thoughtful response. In a research and development project aimed at supporting secondary teachers in implementing formative assessment this is how one teacher summarized her approach to modifying her practice in order to encourage more thoughtful answers from her pupils (Black and Wiliam 2001: 2):

> My whole teaching style has become more interactive. Instead of showing how to find solutions, a question is asked and pupils given time to explore answers together.
>
> Unless specifically asked pupils know not to put their hands up if they know the answer to a question. All pupils are expected to be able to answer at any time even if it is an 'I don't know'.
>
> Pupils are comfortable with giving a wrong answer. They know that these can be as useful as correct ones. They are happy for other pupils to help explore their wrong answers further.

The teachers in the study found that they eventually spent more time and effort in framing questions that would explore issues that were critical to their pupils' development of understanding the subject matter (p. 3). They shifted from their originally more typical closed question and answer style of interaction and presentation to one of exploration of ideas. The learners eventually came to realize that their learning depended less on getting the right answer and more on their willingness to discuss their understanding.

There are further strategies and approaches associated with the dialogic classroom that help pupils to close the gap between what they can do and what they need to be able to do, and we discuss these in future chapters.

## Conclusion

In this chapter we have focused on the need to support learners in coming to know the basis of how their work is judged by their teachers and other assessors. One inescapable aspect of this process is pupil talk, whether in pairs, small groups or the whole class. We have made the case for more dialogue and pupil participation in learning and assessing, and we have offered some suggestions on how teachers might promote pupil understanding of their own learning. In the following chapters we focus on various curricular areas in order to exemplify further the approaches that teachers might use to maximize their pupils' involvement in the assessment dialogue.

# 6   Formative Assessment and Literacy

## Introduction

Literacy is a key medium through which pupils access the curriculum, and as pupils progress through the education system reading and writing assume greater significance as mediums of learning. It is arguable that competence in literacy is one of the most important aims of schooling. The introduction of the Literacy Hour into primary classrooms is an attempt to highlight the importance of literacy, not just as part of the subject, English, but as a medium of learning. In order to maximize achievement in literacy, pupils' progress needs to be assessed in a way that furnishes worthwhile evidence that can be used by learners themselves and by all those seeking to support their development. In this chapter we discuss the kind of assessment that teachers and learners can use to inform the next steps of learning. We will detail some of the assessment procedures for literacy that comply with the ideas about assessment for learning that we have been developing in previous chapters. The distinction we made earlier between planned formative assessment and interactive formative assessment will be revisited here.

We now know that learning cannot be assessed absolutely accurately, reliably and objectively as was assumed in the old psychometric paradigm where measurement in the form of grades and scores reigned supreme. As Gipps (1994a) says, assessment is not an exact science. The upshot of this contemporary view of learning and assessment is not that we should abandon attempts to provide evidence of achievement – transparency of judgement is important and needs to be demonstrated. What it does imply is that there is no such thing as finite assessment or a perfect or infallible assessment. Teachers need information about learners that is multidimensional, drawn from a variety of sources and contexts, and that illuminates the learning process. And even more importantly, as demonstrated in Chapter 5, learners need information about their learning that helps them to improve. How do we assess literacy in a way that furnishes evidence that is useful to both learners and teachers?

## Two scenarios

Consider the following scenarios.

> Pupils in Classroom A are engaged in a wide variety of reading and writing experiences, projects, book talks, conferences and workshops. In conjunction with these activities the pupils keep journals in which they discuss their reflections, including their goals and self-assessment of their achievements. Each pupil keeps a log of their reading and writing activities, as well as a folder that contains lots of samples of their writing. Portfolios are used to keep track of the key aspects of their work over time. During teacher conferences with the pupils, the teacher encourages them to discuss what they have achieved and want to pursue further. The teacher keeps informal notes on what is occurring – attending to different aspects drawn from a menu of possibilities that the teacher and some colleagues have developed. The menu supports but does not constrain the notes the teacher keeps about the pupils. As part of the process, these notes are shared with the pupils, who are encouraged to add their own comments to them. Both the teacher and the pupils refer back to these notes, portfolios etc. to remind themselves of and share what has occurred.

> The students in Classroom B are engaged in a wide range of activities but are not encouraged to monitor themselves. Periodically the teacher distributes a checklist to each pupil with a preset list of skills that the child has to check. Likewise the teacher may interrupt the flow of activities and check the pupils in terms of these preset skills. The skills on the list bear some relationship to some things that are done, but there is a host of things that are not included and some other things that are included that do not seem to be relevant. The listing of skills was not developed by the teacher nor is it open-ended. Instead the list was developed by a curri-

culum committee for the whole country. In some ways the list reflects a philosophy and approach that do not match the current situation. Nonetheless the teacher is expected to keep the checklist and file it. After the checklist is completed and filed it is not re-examined or revised.

These scenarios are offered by Robert Tierney (1998: 375–6) to distinguish between what he calls 'assessment that begins from the inside rather than outside the classroom'. In this book we are seeking to support teachers in engaging in the kind of assessment that originates within the classroom – an inside-out approach to use Tierney's term. Such an approach fits well with all the points we have been making so far about involving the learner in the assessment process. An inside-out approach does not involve overly rigid predetermined criteria regarding what should be looked for and it does not limit the types of learning to be examined. Above all, assessment involves the teacher and learners in negotiation. Tierney suggests that the second example only gives the illusion of being inside-out – in reality, he says it perpetuates what he calls the outside-in approach. Although the teacher uses informal assessment approaches they do not fit with or emerge from the classroom. Also there is little or no negotiation between the teacher and the pupils. We will now suggest a number of ways of assessing literacy in the classroom that have the potential to maximize the participation of the learner. First a note about literacy itself.

## Literacy as complex

Methods used to assess literacy should map onto what we believe literacy is as well as current theory about how literacy is learned (Hall 2003). We know that literacy is complex and multifaceted. Reading is about being able to decode the words on the page, being able to interpret word meanings and grammatical structures. It is about being able to use, reflect on and critique what is read in a meaningful way; it is about what is chosen (and not chosen) to be read and knowing when to read. It is about how and why the reader reads and it is about time devoted to reading, types of texts read, responses to what is read and the variety of genres read. It is about understanding the purposes and intended audiences of texts, about being able to recognize devices used by writers to convey messages and to influence readers, and about being able to make sense of texts by relating them to the situations in which they appear. A parallel list could be made for writing. Reading and writing must be assessed in all this complexity. In addition, and as we noted in Chapter 1, accessing the learner's mind is far from a straightforward matter. To take account of all these points, evidence about a learner's literacy development should be multi-task, multi-mode and multi-contextual. In other words, the learner should be assessed on several literacy tasks, in a variety of modes and in a range of contexts. Some examples follow.

## Literacy assessment approaches

Table 5.1 offers an overview of some literacy assessment approaches, identifying the source of evidence for various elements of achievement and noting

**Table 5.1** Examples of literacy assessment approaches

| Source of evidence | Target aspect of literacy | References |
| --- | --- | --- |
| Miscue analysis and retelling Running record Cloze procedure | Reading strategies, cueing systems, reading fluency, comprehension | Arnold 1982; Clay 1985; Goodman et al. 1987; Moon, 1990; Barrs et al. 1992; Au 1994; Tompkins 1997 |
| Language and literacy conferences Observational/anecdotal records Self- and peer assessments Grids/checklists, reading scales | Awareness of the reading and writing process and attitudes to literacy as well as understanding of what counts as success as a reader/ writer in different contexts; experience as a reader and writer across the curriculum | Barrs et al. 1992; Darling-Hammond et al. 1995; Au et al. 1997; Tompkins 1997 |
| Questioning and observation | Reading and writing processes/strategies | Torrance and Pryor 1998; Cowie and Bell 1999 |
| Portfolios Response journals Self- and peer assessments Essays Book reports Oral and written retellings Drawings and photos | Response to reading: interpretation/ understanding; engagement with different audiences for writing; texts for different purposes | Valencia 1990, 1998; Barrs et al. 1992; Johnston 1992; Valencia and Place 1994; Darling-Hammond et al. 1995; Harrison et al. 1998; Murphy et al. 1998 |
| Profiles/reading indicators Reading benchmarks Descriptive reading scales | Extent to which curriculum content/outcomes or performance goals have been met | QCA/SCAA exemplification material; Barrs et al. 1992 |
| Portfolios Log books, booklists | Breadth and nature of reading (and writing) | Valencia and Place 1994; Leshe and Jett-Simpson 1997; Murphy et al. 1998 Klenowski, 2002 |

some key published accounts of the use of those particular devices. The list is more illustrative than exhaustive. Brief reference will be made to major approaches in the remainder of this section.

### Miscue analysis and retelling

This is a procedure for analysing how children use different cueing systems (grapho-phonic, syntactic and semantic) and strategies (initiating, predicting, confirming) as they read a text aloud. Originally based on the work of Kenneth and Yetta Goodman in the USA, it has since been adapted by others (e.g. Arnold 1982; Moon 1990). A running record is similar in focus (Clay 1985). Both procedures are observation-based and assess reading directly – they take account of the situational specificity of reading knowledge as the performance of the reader is intertwined with the genre of the text being read, the reader's knowledge of the theme of the text, the reader's familiarity with the text, the illustrations in the text, its length and other linguistic features (Murphy *et al.* 1998). Both procedures involve the observation, recording and evaluation of 'errors' a child makes while reading aloud and a judgement about how well the child understands the text.

In practice, an oral reading assessment of this kind requires that a pupil read aloud while the teacher makes annotations of the differences between the text as read and the text as written. The underlying assumption is that the miscues the reader makes offer insights into the range and efficiency with which they apply the range of cues and strategies. The outcome of the assessment is both a descriptive and interpretive/evaluative account of the reader's strategies while reading. The merit of the descriptive-interpretive distinction is that interpretation is tied to data, thus providing transparency – a feature that is much more challenging in documenting reading than it is in writing.

### Cloze procedure

This is an informal tool for assessing comprehension. The teacher selects an excerpt of say 300 words from a text – informational book, textbook or storybook. Then s/he deletes say every fifth word in the passage and the task for the pupils is to use their knowledge of the topic or narrative, of word order in English and of the meaning of words within sentences, to decide on the missing words in the passage. Variations on this procedure include deleting the content words, deleting phrases or even whole sentences. Pupils work in groups or individually and discuss and justify their selections. In the case of those children who may be the focus of the assessment, the teacher observes the meaning-making strategies they use. The advantage of this approach over more traditional question and answer comprehension questions is that it expands on the idea of comprehension so that it involves reconstructing, responding to or interpreting a text rather than merely answering questions about it.

## Language and literacy conferences

In practice the literacy conference can take a variety of formats. Some see the literacy conference as synonymous with any interaction between teacher and pupils about texts. Barrs *et al.* (1992), on the other hand, view this as a more specific procedure. Their book, *The Primary Language Record*, suggests that teachers conduct two conferences per year with each pupil – one in the autumn term, the other in the summer term. The purpose of a conference is to give the child an opportunity to talk about and discuss with the teacher their interests and achievements as a language user. It is suggested that it should be a continuation of 'an already existing dialogue between the child and teacher, as a means of establishing, in a more structured way, children's views of themselves as language learners and language users in and outside school' (Barrs *et al.* 1992: 14). Together the child and the teacher may discuss specific pieces of work and shared experiences, and plan ahead. This should allow time to discuss the child's own perceptions of their strengths and weaknesses. The teacher records decisions arrived at during the conference (see Barrs *et al.* 1992 for examples).

## Portfolios

Portfolios can take different forms: a simple individual folder of work including lists of books read and discussed; written responses to literature or other experiences; non-fiction writing; drawings or paintings in response to a variety of experiences; final pieces and drafts of work in progress. They may also include anecdotal records and observations made by teachers (and others) of pupils during readers' workshops and lessons. Valencia (1990) advocates including a variety of items in the portfolio so that it offers a comprehensive portrayal of the pupil's growth in literacy. Valencia and Place (1994) talk about different kinds of portfolio – the 'showcase portfolio', for example, may be used to display the pupil's best or favourite pieces of work; 'documentation portfolios' capture the pupil's growth over the year; while 'process portfolios' capture the steps taken by a pupil to complete a given project and usually contain pupil reflections on their own learning.

Creating and managing a portfolio takes time. The teacher needs to set aside time to meet with pupils individually to review their portfolios – this could be part of an individual reading conference (see above). Portfolios can be used as public documents, providing concrete examples of the pupil's accomplishments and areas for further development that can be shared with parents and other teachers. Pupils themselves can review their progress over time, take pride in their achievements and make plans for future learning. Portfolios struggle to make reading visible – in our view they are much better for writing than for reading.

## Indicators, benchmarks, scales and checklists

These can take different forms and be used for different purposes. For example, 'level descriptions' are scaled indicators of achievement developed for the National Curriculum. They are summary prose statements that describe the types and range of performance which pupils working towards a particular level of the National Curriculum should demonstrate. There is a scale of eight levels, designed to facilitate progression, for reading, writing, and listening/speaking. Such indicators provide teachers with a supportive framework for describing, recording and reporting their pupils' achievements in literacy – i.e. for summative assessment. These statements also provide a vehicle for ongoing, formative assessment.

However, as we argued in some detail in Chapter 5, any assessment criteria or set of indicators will need to be interpreted by those who use them. As Dylan Wiliam (1998) has observed in relation to assessment criteria in general, it is a fundamental error to imagine that the words laid down in the statements will be interpreted in the same way by all the teachers who use them. They need to be subjected to an ongoing and collective process of shared interpretations such that their meaning is made manifest. When engaged in unpacking the meaning of achievement indicators, teachers inevitably become more critical of a host of issues pertaining to assessment such as the nature of the evidence, the way the evidence was collected to demonstrate the achievement of the criteria, how much evidence constitutes achievement of an indicator, the amount of support offered the learner, the task context, the motivation of the learner and so on.

But more importantly and in relation to the point emphasized in the previous section about helping learners judge the quality of their own work, it follows that benchmarks and indicators need to be understood by learners too, and not just internalized by teachers. Pupils could be encouraged to write the standards in their own language, to discuss examples of evidence of reading and writing and to discuss what artefact or response would be suitable as evidence of, say, their own response to a text. It is in such discussions and in the sharing of ideas about evidence that learners come to grips with the standards they are aiming for.

In addition, they are learning that the interpretation of evidence is open, that evidence can be contested, that assessment is about values and judgements and it makes these aspects explicit. Parents, too, arguably need to be part of the process of making transparent the evaluative criteria, so that the 'guild knowledge' becomes shared in a community of interpreters. In this way assessment can be seen as socially constructed; that there is no perfect or infallible method. Instead, assessment is merely people working collectively and individually to try to describe what is valued (Murphy *et al.* 1998).

Like indicators, benchmarks and reading scales give an account of what the child can do with increasing ease on the way to developing as a reader. One reading scale for younger children (aged 5–7) detailed in Barrs *et al.* (1992) charts progress on a continuum from dependence to independence, while another scale for older children plots the developing experience of readers and describes how they extend and deepen their competence in reading a range of texts. Along with offering teachers a conceptual framework for understanding pupils' reading development, they help teachers become better observers of children and guide instructional decisions by pointing out the full range of strategies and skills that make up reading proficiency (Falk 1998). Reading scales, profiles and indicators have merit in that they help to provide a shared view of reading among teachers and across classes – this helps teachers become more knowledgeable about the different processes and stages and this, in turn, better equips them to address the different needs of pupils.

### Observational or anecdotal records

These are notes kept by teachers about observations made when pupils are working on various reading tasks (e.g. independent – silent – reading, pupil-led and teacher-led discussions of literature, independent or collaborative writing). Observation times can be planned when the teacher focuses on particular pupils and makes anecdotal notes about those pupils' involvement in literacy events – the focus being on what those pupils do as they read and write. Checklists can speed up this process (Au *et al.* 1997). These notes and checklists help teachers determine which skills and strategies need to be addressed with a group or individual in forthcoming (mini)lessons, or need to be the focus of a discussion/conference. Fluency, independence and confidence when reading may depend on the type of text being read or the social (pair, small group, child and adult) or learning/curricular context itself. Observations need to take place across a range of different contexts and with a range of different texts in order to build up a pattern of a child as a reader.

### Observation and interaction

Shepard (2000) talks about 'dynamic assessment' which allows teachers to provide assistance as part of assessment. This, she argues, does more than help teachers gain valuable insights into how understanding might be extended. It also creates perfectly targeted occasions to teach and provides the means to scaffold next steps. As we explained in Chapter 1, Cowie and Bell (1999) unpack a similar notion when they talk about 'interactive formative assessment', by which they mean the process used by teachers and children to recognize and respond to pupil learning in order to enhance that learning during the activity or task. Assessment and the promotion of learning are therefore not separate activities. In the course of assessing, teachers can mediate the learning there and then in the here and now as opposed to some time in the future. Teacher skill in 'noticing' and 'recognizing' what is significant there and then and being able to 'respond' to pupil thinking there and then are crucial for formative assessment. Interactive formative assessment is characterized by activity that is teacher- and pupil-driven rather than curriculum-driven. The aim is to understand the learner's sense-making.

The strength of the above approaches is their directness – the evidence and results arising from them do not require inferencing back to abilities in context. Instead the competencies are assessed in naturally-occurring contexts. The multiple lines of data that exist in multi-task, multi-contextual assessment allow interpretation by a variety of stakeholders – pupils themselves, teachers and parents. The interpretive community (of which we would see learners themselves as a key part) in such assessments is compelled to decide whether the evidence supports the interpretations drawn (Murphy *et al.* 1998), thus suggesting self- and peer assessment.

Because of the authentic nature of these approaches the issue of transfer of skills and abilities is bypassed. In addition, they involve pupils in their own learning and assessment and they capture pupil development over time and in different situations. They are grounded in the assumption that good teaching comes from teachers' knowledge of their pupils and that teachers need to know their pupils well in order to plan effective learning experiences for them. While the evidence remains partial since all assessments are partial, even contextually valid ones, the above approaches are more in line with contemporary thinking about the complexity of literacy, literacy development and assessment that furnishes useful information for learners.

## Interactive formative assessment

As already noted in Chapter 1, interactive assessment arises out of a learning activity that could not be anticipated in advance. It is the kind of assessment that can potentially occur at any time during an interaction – whether in the context of a whole class, small group, pair or individual with teacher. But we hasten to add that both planned formative assessment of the kind described above for literacy and interactive formative assessment are linked through their purposes. In both cases the purpose is to provide evidence that is useful to the learner (and to the teacher) about progress and about how to make more progress. Engaging in one type does not exclude the other. For example, the use of cloze procedure to assess and teach comprehension can be planned but can also offer opportunities that cannot be predetermined to mediate in the learning of an individual with respect to the topic itself and/or the process of learning (social and personal learning strategies).

The remainder of this chapter refers to types of scaffolding learning that can be part of classroom interaction (Duffy and Roehler 1993; Roehler and Cantlon 1996).

### Offering explanations

John Holt, in his famous book *How Children Fail* (1965), tells the story of how a 5-year-old approached her mother, who was busy in the kitchen, and said, 'Mummy, how do traffic lights work?' Her mother said, 'I don't know, darling. Why don't you go and ask Daddy?' To which the little girl quickly replied, 'I don't want to know *that* much about it'. It seems that the good explainer knows when to 'hold back' and keeps the learner in the driving seat. Explanations are explicit statements adjusted to suit the learner's emerging understandings about what is being learned, about why and when it will be used and how it is used. What is key is that explanations are not mere presentations, like a mini-lecture on traffic lights, that do not take account of the learner's current needs as they understand them.

The following example occurred in an early years classroom where most children's first language was not English. They had been discussing the responsibilities of the author and the listeners during 'author's chair' – where pupils sat and read their compositions to the class or the group (Roehler and Cantlon 1996). 'Author's chair' is a practice recommended by Donald Graves (1991) whereby one chair in the classroom is designated as the author's chair and pupils sit in this special chair to share their writing. The focus is on celebrating completed writing projects, not on revising the composition to make it better. Having listed and agreed the various responsibilities (e.g. the listeners should look at the person who is talking etc.) the teacher provided an explanation about why it was important for listeners to help authors feel comfortable when reading in the author's chair:

> All of those things make the person giving the report feel more comfortable . . . Because if you're giving your report and people are showing you that they are interested and that they like your report, then that makes you more comfortable, doesn't it? And you can say, 'Oh, this is fun, I like sharing this because other people are signalling to me that they'd like to hear it'.

### Inviting pupil participation

The lesson continued and learners were given opportunities to join in the process. The teacher, having provided examples of how to complete the task, invited the pupils to show what they knew and understood. The teacher here is helping the pupils know what it is to be a good author. She invites them to talk about the responsibilities of the author during author's chair:

> *Teacher*: Maybe we should now think about how to behave as the author during author's chair. What do authors do? Would you like to start?
>
> *Tina*: The author sits in the chair and speaks loud and clear.
>
> *Crystal*: The author should not fool around like making faces or having outside conversations.
>
> *Shina*: The author should not be shy and should be brave and confident.

### Verifying and clarifying pupil understandings

When the teacher was happy that the pupils understood the author's responsibilities, she asked them to talk about and draw up a list of the listeners' responsibilities. The pupils offered comments such as, 'The audience may try to show that they enjoyed what the authors said . . . I think that the audience should be ready . . . ready to ask questions or offer or have comments when the author stops sharing'.

Teacher responses here included:

> That's really important, isn't it? It may be one of the most important things about the audience's responsibility that you need to think about. Like 'Oh, I like this part because it reminds me of such and such' or 'I wonder what that means?' Or, 'I wonder what would happen if all those types of things would happen'. It is really fun to share those types of questions and comments.

And in the same sequence of interaction:

> *Pupil*: The audience should be thinking of a comment or question for the author.
>
> *Teacher*: That's a good one too. Sometimes that's hard to do, isn't it? To think and listen at the same time. Okay?
>
> *Pupil*: How do you do that?
>
> *Teacher*: Sometimes people have a piece of paper to jot it down. That's OK too. If you feel like you want to have a piece of paper, then we can do that. So do you think we are ready for author's chair?

As the researchers observe, the interaction in this lesson shows how pupils shared their understandings and how the teacher responses verified those understandings. Effort was recognized and the significant knowledge was highlighted. When clarification was needed the teacher provided it.

Researchers in the USA (Duffy *et al.* 1988; Roehler and Cantlon 1996) outline two further ways in which teachers scaffold their pupils' learning or help learners bridge the gap between what they understand and need to understand. These are modelling of desired behaviours and inviting children to contribute clues. Modelling of desired behaviours was mentioned and exemplified in Chapter 1 in relation to developing children's metacognitive awareness, but the researchers just mentioned suggest two types of modelling. One they label 'think-aloud modelling'. An example of this is an activity in which learners are deciding what is important in a book chapter. The teacher thinks aloud during the lesson about the reasoning she is using. Another is 'performance-modelling' where pupils are shown how to complete a task (e.g. the teacher reads silently as the pupils read silently). DEAR or 'drop everything and read' is a familiar activity in primary classrooms in this country and here the teacher physically demonstrates reading and the pleasure of reading by laughing, smiling etc. Inviting pupils to contribute clues or problem solving involves one or several pupils contributing clues for reasoning through having to solve a problem. Here pupils are encouraged to offer suggestions or clues as to how to solve the problem or complete the task. The teacher and the pupils verbalize the process as they go along.

## Conclusion

All of these approaches add up to a philosophy of teaching that promotes a respect for evidence, a willingness to dwell in uncertainty for a while, to tolerate some confusion. A willingness to tolerate the feelings that go along with learning, to suspend judgements and decisions, to be tentative. Such a philosophy rates enquiry and openness and does not rush learners towards closure and the 'right answer'.

Regardless of the subject matter to be learned, such a philosophy is needed in order to help learners to maximize their learning.

# 7 Formative Assessment and Numeracy

## Introduction

In this chapter we use the National Numeracy Strategy (NNS) as a vehicle for raising awareness of the gap that currently exists between formative assessment theory and classroom practice. We maintain that planned quality classroom assessment and valid formal teacher assessment are both needed if learning is to improve and standards are to be raised for all pupils. This is a theme we return to in Chapter 13. We argue that as much consideration and investment needs to be given to supporting teachers in developing assessment that begins inside as has been devoted to assessment that begins outside the classroom. We refer here to national tests. Policy makers may consider, since the Black and Wiliam review (1998b), that they have done all that is possible by emphasizing the importance of this form of assessment through initial teacher training and recent professional development. However, many researchers and teachers are suspicious of their reasons for doing so; a theme we touched upon in Chapter 2. With testing given such high profile, the reality is that many teachers also pay lip-service to theory but do not have the time for involving pupils in assessment at a level necessary for maximizing learning. As one of the teachers in the case study reported in Chapters 3 and 4 said after studying transcripts of lessons and interviews with pupils:

> I find it quite fascinating to have the opportunity to reflect back on the children's perceptions of what is going on ... and also to get a

different angle ... view, em, on the process which you don't get do you? ... I mean you never get the chance to look at something that's gone ... at the end of the day you have a gut feeling ... that went well ... I think most of the kids got something out of that ... most of them enjoyed it and that's the best you can ever do really ... I think so and so grasped the idea ... we've got to do a bit more on this ... reflecting on our own perceptions ... never get enough time to do any more.

(Burke 2000a: 111–12)

She would not have had this opportunity if a written record had not been made of classroom activities as well as of the perceptions of those involved; processes that were costly both in terms of time and energy.

## The NNS

The handbook *The National Numeracy Strategy* (DfEE 1999: 4) describes numeracy as:

a proficiency which involves confidence and competence with numbers and measures. It requires an understanding of the number system, a repertoire of computational skills and an inclination and ability to solve number problems in a variety of contexts. Numeracy also demands practical understanding of the ways in which information is gathered by counting and measuring and is presented in graphs, diagrams, charts and tables.

Since 1999, most primary schools have been using the NNS for teaching mathematics. By implementing the NNS, schools will fulfil their statutory duty with regard to the National Curriculum for mathematics for Key Stages 1 and 2. The mathematics framework and the NNS are fully aligned. The NNS framework, however, is not statutory. The National Curriculum is, and consists of three elements at Key Stage 1:

- using and applying mathematics (Ma1);
- number and algebra (Ma2);
- shape, space and measures (Ma3).

At Key Stage 2 a fourth element, handling data (Ma4), is added.

Each attainment target has two types of description. First, the programmes of study set out what should be taught during each of the key stages. They form the basis for planning. Second, throughout the programmes of study, links are made to other curriculum areas, for example between mathematics and ICT in Ma3 1b. Here pupils are required to select and use equipment to measure, and the link suggests that pupils could use both digital and analogue devices to measure weight or time.

The level descriptions are a guide to making a judgement about a pupil's attainment. They are usually used at the end of a key stage. At Key Stage 1, for instance, most pupils will be working at Levels 1–3 and, at the end of the key stage, the majority of pupils would be expected to have achieved Level 2. At Key Stage 2, most pupils will be working at Levels 2–5 and, at the end of that stage, the majority of pupils would be expected to have achieved Level 4.

The NNS framework contains yearly teaching programmes for reception to Year 6. For each year group, key objectives are defined, and examples of teaching and learning activities are given. The four key principles of the NNS are:

- direct mathematics lessons every day;
- direct teaching and interactive oral work with the whole class and with groups;
- an emphasis on mental calculation;
- controlled differentiation, with all pupils engaged in mathematics on a common theme.

It would appear that the introduction of the NNS has had a positive effect on primary mathematics teaching. In an evaluation (DfEE 2001) the NNS is reported as having been well received by schools, with more direct, interactive teaching, than in the past, with priority given to pupils' oral and mental skills. Our own experience in schools would confirm this judgement. Teachers like the clarity of the approach and can see the benefits to the pupils. The NNS document does give guidance on what classroom assessment should entail (DfEE 1999: 11):

- assessments are used to identify pupils' strengths and difficulties, to set group and individual targets for them to achieve and to plan the next stage of work;
- assessments include informal classroom observations and oral questioning, regular mental tests and half-termly planned activities designed to judge progress; and
- recording systems give teachers the information that they need to plan and report successfully, but are not too time-consuming to maintain.

Teachers are encouraged to 'question pupils effectively, including as many of them as possible, giving them time to think before answering, targeting individuals to take account of their attainment and needs, asking them to demonstrate and explain their methods and reasons for any wrong answer' (DfEE 1999: 5). Teachers are also directed to share 'teaching objectives with the class, ensuring that pupils know what to do; draw attention to points over which they should take particular care, such as how a graph should be labelled, the degree of accuracy needed when making a measurement, or how work can be set out' (DfEE 1999: 11).

Although a successful strategy, the complexity of implementing formative assessment is not recognized by the above statements. With so few research studies of formative assessment practice in normal classrooms, it is possible that policy makers have been convinced by research based largely on experimental settings without considering that contextual adjustments might be needed for those who seek to use it in regular classrooms.

## Teachers as gatekeepers for formative assessment

Formative assessment is both criterion referenced (subject referenced) and pupil referenced (ipsative). The amount of effort the pupil puts into the work, the context of the work, as well as the amount of progress the pupil has made over time are important variables in this process. The pupil's conceptual ability as well as the relevant criteria will therefore determine the judgement made about the work and the feedback given to the pupil. The importance of this form of assessment is that it is diagnostic for each pupil and as such is an important part of teaching. The pupil may recognize the 'small' ideas as they are developed in a specific activity, but the teacher will recognize the 'bigger' ideas that are intended to help the pupil to make progress (Harlen and James 1997: 373). Confusion may arise from the same criteria being used by the teacher for both formative and summative purposes. The complication in terms of assessment is that while formative assessment is always carried out by the teacher, so is a great deal of assessment for summative purposes. The major difference is that while 'summative assessment ... may be criterion-referenced or norm-referenced, formative assessment is always made in relation to where pupils are in their learning in terms of specific content or skills' (Harlen and James 1997: 370).

It is held that pupils should be involved in formative assessment because it is argued that unless they come to understand their own strengths and weaknesses they will not make appropriate progress (Harlen and James 1997). We would ask the reader, at this point, to consider the following questions while reading an account of an assessment incident recorded in a Foundation Stage classroom:

- does the assessor observe the pupil carrying out a task and judge the pupil's meaning against identified numeracy criteria (assessment of learning); or

- does the assessor try to understand how the pupil makes meaning in the task, and is the assessor concerned with interpreting that meaning on behalf of the learner in the light of what is already known about the learner (assessment for learning)?

---

Ishmael is a 4-and-a-half-year-old Islamic boy, whose family are recent arrivals in Britain. He is at an early stage of learning English. In the lesson observed he is working with a supply teacher and a group of under-5s. He is being taught the concept of 5 by a very experienced white teacher. She has responsibility for working with this group while the reception class teacher undertakes different work with the rest of the pupils. This group is provided with coloured blocks and each child is required to place one block in a pre-drawn grid, then two, three and so on until they complete all the squares on the grid. Learning is by activity, with oral work limited to reinforcing key words using previously prepared cards. The teacher shares the quality criteria with the pupils by demonstration and she assesses understanding of the concept 1, 2, 3, 4, 5 by the pupils being able to fill the grid with the correct number of blocks.

While the other pupils do as they are asked, Ishmael does not always do so. He regularly tries to exchange his single coloured blocks with his neighbour so that his colours match. He plays with the blocks, making symmetrical patterns before he places them on the grid. When the other pupils refuse to cooperate by swapping blocks, Ishmael loses interest in the task and does not complete his grid up to five squares. At no time does the supply teacher try to find out why matching colours are so important to Ishmael. At the end of the session, while the other pupils are assessed as having grasped the concept, the supply teacher recommends that Ishmael is given further practice.

---

As observers of these events we asked about Ishmael's apparent interest in symmetry and preoccupation with matching colours. The supply teacher seemed surprised and admitted not having noticed this, but the class teacher recognized it as a regular feature of Ishmael's behaviour. In the subsequent discussion consideration was given to this trait in Ishmael's learning. If it was related to his culture the teacher recognized that she would need to take this factor into account when providing learning opportunities and in assessing his work in numeracy.

Formative assessment as represented above should be essentially positive in content. It is not purely criterion referenced but considers the progress of each individual pupil. It regards inconsistencies in learning as diagnostic evidence. Validity and usefulness are more important than concern for reliability. It should be apparent to the reader that the supply teacher's judgement of Ishmael was 'assessment of learning' not 'assessment for learning'. She failed to recognize that Ishmael was creating an alternative task to that offered or laid down in the NNS. His class teacher had not considered his previous behaviour significant enough to alert her colleague to his particular interests. As referred to earlier, researchers hold that pupils should be involved in this form of assessment because it is argued that unless they come to understand their own strengths and weaknesses they will not make appropriate progress (Harlen and James 1997). With more pupils like Ishmael, at an early stage of learning English, being educated in mainstream schools in the UK the language barrier can make this difficult to achieve. This does not mean that teachers should not try but rather it highlights the importance of taking note of contextual factors, of making formative assessment records and passing them on to other adults charged with making judgements about pupils' achievement.

As we have seen in the above example, assessment against subject criteria is a recognized part of teaching but it is not always ipsative (pupil referenced) or diagnostic. As Gipps writes, 'any assessment model, policy or programme will only be as good as the teacher who uses it' (1994b: 175–6). Yet when Ishmael's teacher became aware of his working practices there was a cognitive shift to a more diagnostic/ipsative approach. She was suddenly aware that he was using strategies which had not been taught. These strategies were intelligently based on the child's understanding of the world, which is often different from the way it is seen by adults.

## Formative assessment theory and practice

Assessment that begins inside the classroom may be intuitive or planned for (see Chapter 1). If teachers adopt a behaviourist approach assessment is something that they do *to* learners, but if a constructivist approach underpins practice learners are fully involved in the process. Constructivists recognize that:

- pupils make sense of what is asked of them from their present understanding of the subject studied, the learning strategies they are familiar with and their beliefs about themselves as learners;
- there is a danger that teacher assessors often interpret meaning on behalf of the pupils without necessarily understanding the pupils' perspectives;
- ideally there should be a dialogue between the teacher and pupils so that misunderstandings can be addressed at an early stage.

Constructivists understand that the sources of invalidity in assessment are:

- when the language of assessment is different from the language of the person being assessed;
- when tasks lack meaning and cultural relevance;
- when alternative tasks to those intended by the teacher can be re-formulated by the pupil;
- when teaching and curriculum are poorly aligned with assessment intentions;
- when the primary goal of assessment is to measure what learners don't know rather than to find out the areas in which they are capable.

Constructivists also raise important questions concerning the equity of assessment practice:

- What knowledge is being assessed and equated with achievement?
- Is the form, content and mode of assessment appropriate for different groups and individuals?
- How does cultural knowledge mediate an individual's responses to assessment, in ways that alter the construct being assessed (Gipps and Murphy 1994: 14)?
- How do perceptions of sub-groups influence teachers' and pupils' expectations and mediate assessment practice?
- How are assessment outcomes interpreted and used?

Drawing on constructivist theory, researchers offer teachers guidance on what classroom assessment should look like (Black and Wiliam 2001). They identify the teacher's role initially as a mediator between the subject and the pupil before the teacher gradually withdraws from the role, guided by formative assessment information. They highlight the importance of teachers communicating appropriate goals to their learners 'and promoting self-assessment as pupils' work towards them'. Training in cognitive skills and helping pupils to identify learning goals are advocated. Focus skills are identified as planning before acting, listing information needed, knowing when and from where to seek help and reviewing and evaluating one's progress. Black and Wiliam see the pupil's role as actively closing the gap between their present state of understanding and what they have been asked to achieve, understanding the difference between learning and performance goals and being honest in their self-assessment. As part of this process, individual pupils need to understand the reasons for having learning intentions shared with them and for being involved in identifying success criteria in advance of undertaking tasks. They should also understand the importance of reflecting on their own work. Most importantly, however, they should be encouraged to face personal demons, which lurk below the surface and threaten to damage their self-esteem. Finally, Black and Wiliam highlight that pupils, in groups, should understand the social and communal dimensions of learning by externalizing their thoughts through dialogue, which enriches personal understanding and leads to new awareness of their own thinking. In this way pupils should gain the capacity to understand the thinking of others through reasoned interpersonal negotiation, and become aware that this can lead to consensus (even when there cannot be agreement).

## Formative assessment in a Year 6 numeracy lesson

Read the following lesson commentary and as you do so apply theory to practice. Consider the advantages to this teacher and her pupils of a system of well-planned assessment conducted by teachers who know the pupils' strengths and weaknesses, as opposed to the disadvantages of a system based on externally applied tests and primarily planned with native English speakers in mind.

---

**Year 6 (60 minutes)**
**Context**
Twenty-four pupils present out of 26. No classroom assistant present. The room is divided from the next classroom by an ill-fitting sliding screen. Resources include overhead projector. The windows have no blinds.

**Learning intentions**
To practise and develop oral/mental skills. To convert between £s and pence. Main teaching tasks for week: to use number facts and place values to add/subtract mentally; to extend written methods to include addition and subtraction of numbers; to use all four operations (add, subtract, multiply, divide) to solve problems.

**Field notes**
Teacher has a secure knowledge of the NNS; this is evident in her planning, her calm approach to the pupils and in her open-ended questioning which help pupils model themselves on this approach and develop thinking skills. Work is very well planned in line with the NNS. Teacher is very quick with calculations/number work, acting as a very good role model for her pupils. Praise is used well as a feedback strategy to pupils and motivation levels are high. Teacher's regular checking of her notes slows pace of delivery. Evidence of very good emphasis on

---

approaching word problems in maths; worksheets support this line of development and once understanding is secure, calculations prove no difficulty. Key words are identified and displayed. A lot of oral interaction taking place between teacher and pupils. Half of class responds positively that they have been successful in the first problem set. Calculators allowed but pupils have to justify their use. Evidence of good progress over time in workbooks: numerical calculations, shape, use of data and problem solving. Worksheets are planned for all attainment levels. Teacher picks up problem from one group and uses it for a revision session for all. Teacher doesn't ask gifted and talented boy who volunteers answer but puts him on hold by asking him to think how he will explain his reasoning. In meantime she calls on a middle attainer. All senses are stressed as important in answering a problem (e.g. visualizing, thinking aloud etc.). Girl with identified special educational needs has problem dividing by 2. Teacher makes time to help her. Gifted and talented boy (mentioned above) explains his reasoning using an overhead projector slide. One girl has made a mistake and other pupils suggest ways to put it right.

Pupils have obviously been taught well over a period of time because of their confidence with numbers. Gifted and talented pupils can double numbers in their heads easily and accurately up to 2096. Majority of pupils are confident with numbers over 1000. Good strategies taught previously; pupils draw on these to solve present problems.

Overhead projector slide writing is quite difficult to see from the back of the room with no blinds on windows and a very sunny day. Noise through folding screen, from neighbouring class, doesn't help when teacher in this class is insisting on her pupils listening to a word problem. The two gifted and talented boys next to the overhead projector screen concentrate very well in the circumstances.

Pupils all well behaved with no evidence of lack of respect for teacher. Monitors give out worksheets efficiently. Evidence of raised self-esteem with one boy making fist in the air when teacher accepts his solution. Pupils self-check and mark own work. Gifted and talented are all boys. Discussion among gifted and talented is intense particularly in deducing the actual focus of the questions on the worksheets. Only one third of class have been in this school for the whole of their school career. Highly mobile school population.

Teaching has to be very good to move the learning forward because of the number of pupils for whom English is an additional language and who have experienced past disruption to their schooling. All pupils have benefited from learning strategies which they can use in other situations. Problems lie in language understanding, limitations in previous learning experiences and lack of confidence in formal test situations.

Disappointment for teacher and pupils as the head teacher appears at the end of the lesson and shares the fact that the maths SATs results for Year 6 are down by 5 per cent in the school. The staff blame lower than expected results on the obscure language used on the test paper.

## Analysis of field notes

This teacher knows her pupils. Thinking is high profile in this classroom. The teacher models good practice through her confidence with numbers and her use of open-ended questions. She builds in time for reflection, as for example when the gifted and talented boy's contribution is put on hold until a middle attainer has had a chance to contribute. This teacher also recognizes that a pupil's ability to carry out an activity 'is never more than part of what we call "competence". The other part is the ability to monitor the activities. To do the right thing is not enough, one must also know what one is doing and why it is right' (von Glasersfeld 1987: 13). Pupils are encouraged to self-check and self-mark and also to peer support those with learning difficulties. Reasoning is more important in this classroom than getting a correct answer. The teacher described, after the lesson, how her planning had changed that year as a result of her understanding that her pupils needed less time to draw graphs but more time to interpret them. In this way she used formative assessment to inform her planning, which in turn will hopefully improve learning. These pupils are fully involved in assessment and their learning benefits from this degree of involvement. This is evident in the motivation, particularly, of the gifted and talented boys. They are disadvantaged in SATs, however, because they are judged ultimately by assessment that starts outside the classroom.

## Conclusion

Educationalists may not fully know how pupils learn but what is recognized is that real learning cannot be imposed completely but is concerned with individuals making meaning for themselves (see Chapter 1). The individual is a key participant in the sequence of rational actions, thinking, defining and reordering of events which are central features of the self-assessment process (Kolb 1984). The discovery of meaning can only be made by the learner and cannot occur without the involvement of the learner. A critical transformation occurs when a receiver of information or experience is able to interpret the information in terms of their own culture, character, ambitions and learning style. If learners are not given the time and opportunity to examine, consider in context and evaluate their experience and/or information, then understanding may be more limited for only the learner can turn these experiences into a resource, which can have deep significance for them. If, for example, the teacher does not fully share lesson learning objectives or only chooses to give too limited independence of action or application, then the purpose of the learning may not be clear for the learner. It is quite possible, in these cases, for the learner to work to a different set of expectations than those of the teacher and this can lead to misunderstanding, frustration and ultimately lower achievement.

Surely these Year 6 pupils, and others in schools across the country, would be more fairly served by a more formative approach to assessment (Denvir 1989). Tests only give scores on a narrow area of learning; establishing a common meaning for the activities can go further if the teacher is the assessor. If, for example, the pupils' 'expert' knowledge and the meaning of the task are negotiated through discussion before the assessment, the assessors would stand a better chance of gaining information about the children's awareness of:

- the mathematical concepts and procedures which they had grasped;
- the contexts in which these have been experienced and understood;
- the children's' interests, knowledge and expertise in their everyday world, as well as in their school work (Denvir 1989: 283).

This type of assessment is time-consuming for teachers but it serves pupils' interests by allowing teachers more freedom to cover the whole range of learning rather than simply preparing pupils to pass tests, which happens too frequently in schools driven by performance in league tables (Broadfoot 1999). Moderation of results would ensure that they were fair and accurate. We do not call for tests to be abolished but we do believe that a more equal balance of assessments from inside as well as from outside the classroom would offer a more valid basis for understanding and informing pupils' learning than that which currently exists. In the next chapter we continue with this theme as we follow one teacher's metacognitive journey as she plans classroom 'assessment for learning' in science.

# 8 Formative Assessment and Science: Girl-Friendly or Boy-Friendly Context?

## Introduction

In this chapter we look beyond theory, policies and commentaries on practice and observe the changes of mindset that occur as one teacher (second author) plans language support and formative assessment strategies for a process-based science project. The use of this case study material provides a model of the metacognitive process in action as Winifred identifies a problem and tries to plan a programme with the pupils, rather than having the curriculum or the teacher's needs to the fore. In the process she learns about herself and her science colleague's values. She finds the task complex and time-consuming, but while she is changed by the process she has been through, her science colleague's mindset remains much as before.

The Key Stage 1 and Key Stage 2 National Curriculum for science requires that pupils be taught strategies for engaging in scientific enquiry:

- how to plan, obtain and present evidence to support that enquiry;

- to consider the evidence gathered, to evaluate what they have done and to present what they did to others.

The focus for this enquiry is threefold.

1 life processes and living things;
2 materials and their properties;
3 physical processes.

Elements of the English, mathematics and information and communication technology (ICT) programmes of study are identified as being a meaningful part of this process and teachers are expected to plan accordingly.

## The process-based science project: context

At the time of this study I was the deputy headteacher and curriculum leader for English of a 9–13 middle school. In this school pupils in Years 6–8 received specialist teaching. I became aware, through my pastoral responsibility for the children's welfare, that we had a problem that appeared to stem from science lessons. When science lessons were taking place, girls regularly invaded the medical room seeking attention. Linked with the fact that parents were complaining that their children couldn't understand the science homework that was set, I decided to pursue the matter and try to find out what was at the root of the problem. When I approached the science master he complained that the pupils 'lacked understanding and the ability to follow and take work into some written form'. He placed the blame at the English department's door. He felt that pupils were not taught how to make notes or how to structure their writing to support the needs of the science curriculum. The problem had been neatly turned and squarely located by my colleague into my own domain. I agreed to consider the problem and try to draw up a framework to support the pupils' speaking and listening skills in order to improve the quality of their learning and ultimately their written work, as they completed a study of the local river.

## Investigating the world of pupils and teachers

At the time of this project I was studying for a higher degree. Although I recognized that my own English teaching practice drew on a plurality of styles, I had become increasingly aware of and convinced by the theoretical writings of Vygotsky (1987) and Bruner (1989). Following these convictions I decided to engage in 'authentic dialogue' (Freire 1989: 48) with the girls involved, in order to understand their perceptions of science. One example must suffice as representative of many of the middle and lower attainers' views on the subject:

> *Amy:* Science is boring, can't we have art and do our books this afternoon?
> *Teacher:* Aren't you studying the river?
> *Amy:* Oh yes, we're going to be making visits, but at the moment it's all rocks and things.
> *Teacher:* But isn't that interesting? I found it so.
> *Amy:* But you have to remember, which is which, igneous . . .
> *Teacher:* They were formed by fire weren't they?
> *Amy:* I think so but it's hard . . . What's that [pointing]?
> *Teacher:* Oh that's not rock but man-made. It is concrete . . .
> *Amy:* See what I mean? It's difficult.
> [Later when I passed her and her friend they were chanting the names of rock categories]

This pupil was concerned about her own lack of understanding and was capable of generating an example of her own difficulty; yet her science teacher dismissed her thus: 'Amy is not innately interested'. As Barnes writes, behind every utterance lies the 'unspoken backcloth of meaning' and 'children who fail in school are those who operate with ways of meaning different from those of schooling' (1989: 76). As I read the relevant literature and reflected on this problem I realized that no position is completely neutral and that all aspects of schooling are subject to the effects of gender, race and class (Murphy 1989). If I was to understand the girls' science anxieties and address the parents' and science teacher's concerns I recognized that I had to understand not only how the girls constructed their understanding of science but where they saw themselves within that world. I also needed to understand the views held by the boys.

I got permission to accompany a Year 6 class on a science investigation of a local pond. This offered a revealing example of different gender reactions to the task of pond dipping:

> *Natasha:* I'm finding practical work fun [holding her dripping net] . . . I would usually have got information from books . . . but Mr Elson suggested I got out and found more practical methods . . . I was a bit unhappy at first . . . but I find this way fun . . .
> *Billy:* I don't like science at the moment . . . too much biology . . . give me motors and electricity any day.

These two higher-attaining pupils were unaware of my interest in their conversation. They were clearly able to express their ideas and to recognize their own reluctance to follow certain pathways or to become involved in every area of knowledge. I recognized, however, that there are many pupils who are less articulate and whose values are less easy to identify. Interestingly, as I considered my pupils' gender needs I began to recognize gender biases, as a female, in my dealings with my male science colleague that impacted on my discussions concerning my support for the river project. He, for example, always took the lead in any exchange, even when I had initiated the exchange of views. His answers to my questions were always succinct and seemed to allow for no other lines of enquiry. My position by comparison seemed weaker, as I still debated points and allowed room for doubt. Maybe, I argued with myself, if the girls felt the same as I did, by choosing a more girl-friendly speaking and listening activity I would balance the science more in the girls' favour. I considered what might constitute unfriendly science for boys and girls, assisted by Murphy (1989):

- Girl-unfriendly science: physics context, masculine, practical, electrical, multiple choice questions, structural, mechanistic, abstracted single response
- Boy-unfriendly science: domestic context, some biological contexts, response – open-ended and extended, answers concerned with non-structured variables (Murphy 1989).

On the other hand, if I aimed for a task which was not gender-biased I might achieve the best learning from both sexes. Such a task would focus on the use of knowledge rather than abstract explanation. It would have a practical context but not be overtly scientific in terms of equipment and instrumentation. It would be open in as much as it would allow pupils to determine its relevance by testing out and rejecting their own hypothesis in the light of the data collected. Such tasks could also provide the pupils with an opportunity to feel ownership of the problem.

## My planned support for the river study

In the event I chose to support the science study by developing the pupils' speaking and listening skills. The focus for my part of the enquiry was 'how people use and change the river by their usage'; this represented one part of the planned science investigation. It was planned to use one of the English lessons per week over a period of six weeks. The aim for Activities 1–5 was to plan, obtain and present evidence to support a scientific enquiry.

### Activity 1 (discussion)

What do pupils already know about how the local people use the river?

1    Collect children's ideas (groups).
2    Share experiences, focusing on recurring ideas and developing categories of use for Activity 3 (groups).
3    Self-reflect on individual performance (talk diaries and evaluation sheets, contributions made, feelings about working in this way).

### Activity 2 (water board video)

1    Provide pupils with worksheet highlighting how they can become more efficient in listening for key points and in making notes from a video; in particular directing them to considering the linguistic code of interviewing as a means of collecting information.
2    View video and make notes in talk diaries (stop video regularly, use freeze frame and playback).
3    Reflect on information considered important by pupils, on how interviewing was used and how successful the pupils thought it had been in securing the information sought.

### Activity 3 (purposeful focusing in groups)

1    Divide class into groups ensuring a good social, gender and attainment mix.
2    Allow groups to select leaders, secretaries and monitors of performance.
3    Allocate categories identified in Activity 1 and allow groups to choose the subject for their investigation as well as who in the locality they feel might best answer their questions.
4    Compose letter explaining what the project is about and ask the chosen interviewee for permission at a time convenient to both parties to interview them, offering examples of the types of question that might be asked.

### Activity 4 (groups)

1    Refine purpose of interview.
2    Consult books.
3    Plan questions.
4    Devise interview schedule including method of recording information.

5    Role play being interviewer and interviewee.
6    Define success criteria as class and write them up on the board.

## Activity 5 (interviews in groups)

1    Everyone to know their role within the task (asking questions, working tape recorder, checking schedule).
2    Welcome visitor.
3    Follow schedule as planned.
4    Thank visitor.
5    Reflect on the displayed success criteria.

The next aim was to consider the evidence gathered, to evaluate what had been achieved and to present the results to others.

## Activity 6 (self- and peer assessment)

1    Allocate tasks and work in pairs to draft a report explaining to the science teacher what evidence of river usage has been gathered, how successful or otherwise the pairs thought they had been and what they might change if they could start again.
2    Use computers, tape recorders or normal writing equipment to present the published report to the science teacher.

In Activity 1 I was placing school knowledge in a setting of everyday happenings. By emphasizing ownership of the work I was recognizing that 'different experiences pupils have out of school do not lead only to differences in their skills but more importantly to differences in their understanding of situations and problems in which their skills can be used appropriately' (Murphy 1989: 327). In other words, I was recognizing that values determine the problems we perceive and the solutions we find acceptable. By scaffolding the pupils in the way I planned I hoped to redress the balance and ensure that they not only understood what was presented and asked of them but that they would be able to take the work into an appropriate written or other self-chosen form. The river study was only a vehicle for my central concern, which was the development of procedural and conceptual knowledge in my pupils.

As a teacher I could only theorize and plan on my present understanding and previous experiences. I recognized the need to have a clear vision of content and the process to follow, otherwise I would be exhibiting 'brute sanity' rather than 'informed wisdom' (Fullan 1989: 156). By choosing group work as my main form of organization I expressed my belief that conflict plays a part in moving learners towards an objective rather than a subjective approach to a problem (Hoyle 1989) – for example, in the discussion of interview techniques. I envisaged myself joining groups by observing activities, intervening if necessary to focus thinking or keep pupils on track. In doing so, however, I recognized the need to be sensitive to the social pattern within the group, including the pattern of dominance, which might impede or facilitate learning. Finally I aimed for a coherent teaching identity related to pedagogy, style and approach to the areas of knowledge covered, because in my experience pupils need to feel that they can rely upon their teacher and operate comfortably within the classroom.

In reflecting on this programme I am aware that by adopting a social constructivist stance, I placed emphasis on the pupil as a constructor of their own learning. I also valued both peer group and pupil/teacher interaction in informing and facilitating the learning process (Wood 1988: 226). I realize, however, that I still retained aspects of earlier theoretical positions, as I limited my pupils to one form of linguistic 'code' (interviewing) and could be accused of pursuing my educational aims and not sufficiently considering my pupils' views. Equally, while I aimed to liberate my pupils following Vygotsky's advice that instruction should be aimed not so much at the ripe but the ripening functions, my pupils might be locked, through previous experience in science, into looking for the right answer rather than being able to take risks. Consider again the example of Amy as she tried to commit rock categories to memory.

## My formative assessment strategies

My aims in the development programme were twofold:

1  to establish a more pupil-centred learning experience;
2  to furnish teachers with information which would help them to pitch the learning experience within each pupils' zone of proximal development (Wood 1988: 25).

The outcomes I was looking for were:

- the pupils' ability to organize their own learning in groups;
- evidence of task involvement;
- evidence of perceptual awareness, speculation, imagination and hypothesizing;
- conceptual change.

In considering these outcomes I valued the individual as a maker of meaning who uses an inherited language in order to make meaning in community with other human beings with similar knowledge, interests and values. I also recognized that 'speech expresses both the speakers ... experience of the world and the inner world of consciousness' (White and Gorman 1989: 313) and I placed emphasis on what the pupils themselves perceived. Finally I recognized that learners have different solutions to the same task and that these are indicative of present understanding. I believe in the collaborative nature of pupil/teacher continuous assessment and so laid emphasis on formative assessment *for* learning rather than formative assessment *of* learning.

## Pupil self-assessment

The first part of the planned self-assessment sheet was to be filled in by each pupil at the end of Activity 1 and the second part after Activity 6. This assessment was concerned with two aspects of learning in groups. In the first instance, pupils were asked to evaluate their own oral contributions to the group:

- Able to join in discussion with my group     1 2 3
- Can make suggestions as to how to tackle the task facing my group     1 2 3
- Can listen carefully to what others say without being distracted 1 2 3
- Can listen to the views of others and then compare them to my own     1 2 3
- Can give ideas and opinions which take the discussion forward and do not go off the point     1 2 3

Later they were asked to evaluate how they reconsidered their ideas in the light of what they had learned from the project:

- Can change my mind when persuaded by the good ideas of others     1 2 3
- Can stick to my own ideas or opinions when I am sure of them 1 2 3
- Can report back to the rest of the class     1 2 3
- Can encourage others to take part     1 2 3
- Can sum up what has been said so far to help the group     1 2 3
  Key: 1 good   2 satisfactory   3 poor

Pupils with reading difficulties would be helped by the teacher and a note of help given attached to the form. This was a criteria-referenced assessment with the criteria generated by myself as the teacher.

## Teacher's formative assessment

This schedule was designed to focus teacher assessment on the individual who might be a cause for concern within a group situation. It allowed for the collection of factual data (name, date, context etc.) as well as a subjective response (yes/no) to the eight defined sets of criteria listed below, supported by commentaries and/or examples of speech. The pupil's behaviour on the task could be sampled at various times during the programme to check for any evidence of change (e.g. following teacher intervention).

- Does the pupil take turns or frequently talk over or interrupt?
- Does the pupil contribute, invite others' contributions, redirect contributions and encourage others?
- Does the pupil listen to others? Do they show a willingness to learn from others by their response and reactions to others' contributions?
- Does the pupil indulge in 'parallel' talk (i.e. continue their own line of thinking or integrate their own ideas with others)?
- Does the pupil elaborate an answer rather than answer in monosyllables? Do they give details of events, people and feelings or provide reasons, explanations or examples?
- Does the pupil extend ideas rather than let ambiguity go unchallenged? Do they do this by asking for specific information or by asking for clarification?
- Does the pupil explore suggestions by asking for alternatives or by speculating, imagining and hypothesizing?
- Does the pupil take part in evaluation by pooling ideas? Do they suspend judgement before making choices?

## Justification of use of formative assessment

By giving pupils greater ownership of their learning I hoped to cut down the number of task reluctance factors identified at the start of the study. I hoped the teacher assessment schedule would help me to gain understanding of less confident learners so that I could do some direct teaching of study skills in order that they could take a fuller part (Watts and Bentley 1989).

I would be addressing three kinds of question about my pupils' learning:

1 Where is this pupil now?
2 How can I help this pupil further?
3 What questions does this raise about the learning opportunities I am providing and how might these facilitate progress in science?

The information gained should:

- inform my own practice and my pupils' learning;
- act as a focus for staff discussion;
- enter my record keeping system (may prove useful in my discussions with parents);
- provide evidence of my assessment approach for the headteacher and outside agencies.

These proposals were limited in their usefulness to my own pupils and circumstances. Desmond Nuttall writes, 'every assessment is based upon a sample of the behaviour in which we are interested'. Any generalization from this particular behaviour must be seen in terms of the 'universe of that behaviour' (Nuttall 1989: 265). In order for this to take place the 'universe' has to be carefully defined to embrace the conditions and occasions of the assessment as well as the content. For assessment is judged in terms of:

- Validity: does this assessment investigate what it sets out to achieve?
- Reliability: is this investigation repeatable, using another assessor or another occasion; is it of any value?
- Utility: embracing the convenience, flexibility and inexpensiveness of assessment.

In the setting (universe of behaviour) of the river study, I expressed a clear idea of what I wanted to assess (the pupils' responsibility for their own learning and how they expressed their feelings through speaking and listening – the construct). I used more than one method and source of gathering data to ensure validity. I tested out both assessment schedules ahead of the study and felt reasonably satisfied that both pupils and staff felt confident in their use. Finally, in considering 'utility' in my programme, I tried to strike a balance by involving everyone in the assessment process, thus making it a collaborative part of the study rather than being seen as an appendage tacked on at the end.

In reflecting on the programme I recognize that I was assessing the procedural and conceptual knowledge of the pupil in order to determine progress and future potential. When pupils are working in groups I was interested in composition, organization and interaction in order to determine the effect on learning.

## Reflection on the planned proposals

In retrospect I realize that the question I chose to ask and the way I planned to present the task to the pupils altered the information available. I could have used a practical demonstration for my introductory activity in response to the more personal question, 'How much water do we each use on average every day?' As the teacher, I knew from my reading that this is between 150 and 500 litres. If I had provided 15 10-litre buckets, each filled to the brim, I would have had a graphic example of minimum daily usage; on the other hand, I might have had problems obtaining the buckets. I would have involved the pupils, but I would only have 'found out' the answer to a problem for which I already knew the answer. In other words, I would have been guiding my pupils towards an already identified goal rather than allowing them to construct new knowledge.

By posing the question I did, however ('How do people use and change the river by their usage?'), I was aware that my pupils might not interpret it as I did. I generated the question and I restricted the linguistic code to interviewing. In retrospect I could have allowed the pupils to generate the question and allowed them more flexibility in the programme (e.g. a survey to monitor local pollution). Clearly, although I claimed to recognize that the best learning comes from the pupils' attempts to make sense of their own experiences, I still clung to earlier held behaviourist tendencies as I planned topics which arose from the wisdom of the curricularist and not the curiosity of the learner (Watts and Bentley 1989).

I was more satisfied with my choice of formative assessment procedures. By choosing continuous assessment and involving pupils in self-assessment practices I signalled that I valued the pupils' achievements by regarding them as apprentices who were journeying towards expert competency. As an English teacher I was used to accepting different modes of expression, and as long as pupils addressed the issues and related them to genre and audience I valued their contributions. My main concern was that my science colleague was not working from the same theoretical stance as myself. He interpreted differences in pupils' expression as differences in achievement or ability rather than as opportunities to understand where the pupils were coming from so that he could engage with the learners at that point. I recognized that his was a transmission mode of teaching rather than a facilitative one. Assessment was something he regarded as his domain and not something he shared with the pupils. There was a wide gap to be filled at the level of theoretical beliefs and this led to the identified problem, which emerged from our practice.

# Conclusion

The purpose, which I highlighted in my planning for this science study, was the development of procedural and conceptual skills through speaking and listening in groups. This was planned to address an identified mismatch between what pupils could do in English lessons and what they transferred with them into science. If this purpose was to be satisfied, however, greater liaison needed to occur between domains, as a regular feature of practice.

Following reflection on my planning, I would now change the emphasis on interviewing as the only means of collecting information. In making this change I would allow groups of pupils more freedom to choose their investigation techniques. Computer programmes could be used for analysing, creating graphs and presenting data. By opening up the programme, however, I would be creating more resourcing and organizational problems in matching pupils to tasks and managing group activities. However, the gains should outweigh the pressures. What is more worrying is that now politicians have considerable powers over curriculum control, investigative assessment of this type may be swamped by grading, ranking, rating, sorting and classifying by test results and accountability. As a reflective teacher I believe that preparing a better approach to assessment is a task teachers need to address.

### Retrospective view

This programme was planned for an Open University masters' degree course in 1990. Thirteen years later, while more is known about assessment for learning, as is evident in the preceding and following chapters, teachers are still struggling to achieve the right balance between 'assessment of learning' and 'assessment for learning'. The difference now is that formative 'assessment for learning' is recognized as something that teachers need to get right. Changes of policy that are positively affecting practice, such as those recorded in Chapter 11, offer hope for the future.

# 9 Art and Design and Formative Assessment: 'How can you get a "C" on a coat-hanger sculpture?'

## Introduction

In this chapter we consider art and design education in terms of the creative growth of the learner and assessment in the context of the quality of education schools offer pupils. Literacy and numeracy strategies have been considered in Chapters 6 and 7 as posing problems for the implementation of formative assessment for learning. Art and design, being concerned with the personal expression of the individual, would seem to offer a more fertile ground for involving pupils. Being a foundation rather than a core subject, like history in Chapter 10, it also receives less interference from policy makers, and teachers in principle are freer to plan the curriculum and assessment opportunities they offer pupils. Examples from our field notes are used in this chapter to share current practice. Discussion will centre on the teaching and possible mindsets of two primary teachers, as well as the learning that is observed as they deliver cultural aspects of the art and design curriculum.

## The teacher and the art and design curriculum

The National Curriculum for art and design in the foundation stage and primary years requires that pupils receive a broad and balanced experience of two- and three-dimensional tasks including the use of computer-generated art and research using electronic sources. QCA exemplars support schools in planning and providing relevant art experiences. The recommended teaching of knowledge, skills and understanding should include:

- exploring and developing ideas;
- investigating and making art, craft and design;
- evaluating and developing work;
- knowledge and understanding.

The fact that most children are taught by one teacher or a comparatively small number of teachers in the infant and primary school should allow for a rounded view of an individual child's experience and progress. Flexibility in balancing time between various activities over the course of a week would seem a possibility. The introduction of the subject-dominated National Curriculum did ensure that schools had to provide a broad curriculum for all children regardless of the school they attended. This did not, however, ensure consistency in the quality of what was covered or consistency in assessment practice, because teachers' mindsets are determined more by previous experiences and personal understanding than external pressures.

In order to focus adequately on the literacy and numeracy strategies, starting in September 1998, schools were allowed more freedom in their delivery of the foundation subjects with the exception of ICT and RE (religious education). Although this has now been suspended, art and design education in many schools suffered in favour of the literacy and numeracy focus. Sound art and design education requires insight into the nature of art experience and understanding of the development of children, their visual and tactile imagery, and the qualities and potential of materials. It is recognized that not all primary teachers have the flair for, or understanding of, art and design and as a result may offer the children they teach a lightweight experience, which fails to extend or stimulate them. Yet the responsibility for most of the children's art and design experiences resides with them rather than their secondary colleagues. For the majority of children, formal art and design education ceases by the age of 14!

## Relating theory to practice

Teachers are required, as referred to above, to deliver an art and design curriculum which extends pupils' knowledge, skills and understanding. If they adopt a behaviourist model they plan activities without taking any account of pupils' prior knowledge and understanding, believing in the main that learning is a response by the learner to the stimuli presented to them. While this is probably an adequate explanation of simple knowledge, it fails to account for complex learning. If teachers choose to adopt a constructivist model, however, they are taking greater risks by sharing power more equally with their pupils and as a result have to be more confident to handle the open-ended learning situations which may arise.

Much in the constructivist view of teaching and learning may be traced back to John Dewey's (1934) notion of children as holistic learners. Teachers in Dewey's view need to be not so much knowledge givers as learning enablers, by which he meant providers of experiential opportunities. From Johann Pestalozzi (1746–1827) to Maria Montessori (1870–1952) learning theorists have stressed that teaching and learning is best accomplished by finding ways for children to experience new information first hand and thereby both to assimilate and accommodate that knowledge. It was, after all, Pestalozzi who stated that the impressions gained through the senses are the foundation of instruction.

Let us look at two art and design lessons, delivered by primary teachers, and consider how these teachers can know what the pupils have learned. This assessment question is after all at the heart of constructivist teaching. As you read, consider:

- *What knowledge and understanding have the pupils constructed as a result of instruction and experience?*

I would suggest that this is a different question from

- *Did the pupils learn the prescribed knowledge?*

Or

- *Do the pupils now understand in the manner that I (or the curriculum) have set up as ideal (or satisfactory or competent)* (Walling 2000: 62)?

## Year 4 art and design lesson

The National Curriculum requires that pupils are given opportunities to develop an appreciation, critical awareness, knowledge and understanding of the work of other artists, designers and craftspeople from their own and other cultural heritages. In planning a series of lessons based on art and crafts from different cultures, a Year 4 teacher has drawn inspiration from a very good resource book that supports her knowledge and understanding of these cultures. It includes examples of 'how to do' crafts, for use with children. The pupils have already, over a number of weeks, made African masks, Aborigine dream paintings and American Indian dream catchers.

In the introductory session to this lesson one quarter of the pupils take part in demonstrating orally their knowledge and understanding of the previous cultures studied. They respond correctly to the teacher's closed questions (mainly concerned with technical words associated with each culture), while the others remain silent (refer to Chapter 5 p. 52). The teacher tells the class that the objective for this lesson is to learn to make Ikat weaving. She does not give a visual example of what this form of weaving is like by way of pictures or artefacts, or explain its unique qualities. She simply states that it is another world craft. The class is taught two new technical words, 'weft' and 'warp', and what they mean, reinforcing in the pupils' minds that this literacy information is important to the teacher and is worth remembering. This is followed by a demonstration by the teacher of how to make a wool warp on a card frame by securing the wool ends with masking tape and tensioning the warp by stretching the wool through parallel grooves cut at either end of the rectangular piece of card. Only one colour of wool is available although Ikat is a highly complex and decorative form of weaving. The pupils make the warps easily but have problems with weaving the weft because they only have their fingers as tools for holding the wool. The teacher explains to the observer that only five bodkins are available and that rather than advantaging a few pupils a decision has been made not to give any out. Very quickly a number of pupils start to feel inadequate and say that they can't do the task (an example of 'learned helplessness' – refer to Chapters 4 and 5). A few pupils have poor left/right coordination and keep doubling back on themselves before completing a line. Noise levels rise and social chatter prevails, except at one table where a boy with previous weaving experience has devised a means of controlling his weft by using two pencils. He weaves over these every time he reaches either end of a line and the quality of his weaving is evident for his peers to see. It is neater, more controlled and looks like a piece of cloth. Very

> soon other pupils near him copy his example. Having benefited from his re-
> sourcefulness in learning, they too learn to control the weft.

## Formative evaluation

This teacher has a problem in setting up this lesson in that she hasn't got enough tools for the task. If her approach had been more constructive she might have shared her problem with the pupils. She could have, for example, asked them how they could use offcuts of the thick cardboard, left from producing the weaving frame, to develop a tool that would hold the wool more efficiently than their fingers could. In this way she would have involved the pupils more and self-esteem might have been raised rather than lowered, as turned out to be the case. Also, by limiting the pupils to a single colour of wool (white) the teacher took away the essential quality of Ikat weaving, which relies on the threads being arranged in bands of colour for stripes or checks. She did tell the pupils the learning intention, which was to make an Ikat weaving, but not what it involved. She made organizational decisions which limited the pupils' ability to make decisions for themselves. The majority of pupils failed to make a simple piece of weaving. A few succeeded thanks to the one boy who proved so inventive with the pencils.

As educators we did not recognize what Ikat weaving was from this encounter and feel sure that the pupils did not either. The low expectations on the teacher's part led to low self-esteem and the fear of failure on the part of a number of pupils, while others were complacent that they had succeeded when in actual fact they had achieved no more than might be expected (Barber 1996). We would suggest that this exposure to world crafts could seriously damage pupil interest. Yet if the teacher had been more knowledgeable about art education and confident enough to adopt a constructivist approach, her recognition of the need to share clear learning intentions and involve pupils in identifying the success criteria ahead of working might have helped her to create a better learning environment.

## Year 6 art and design lesson

The National Curriculum for art and design stresses that pupils should be taught about the visual/tactile qualities of materials/processes and the manner in which they can be manipulated and linked to ideas/purposes/audiences. In this lesson, with a Year 6 class, the teacher is encouraging pupils to work in groups and experience practical methods by gaining knowledge and understanding of Monet's style of working, as well as to research Greek culture for their current topic by using computers. The lesson follows a period of time when SATs preparation has dominated the curriculum and the teacher has promised the pupils more opportunity for creative expression and research. She is adopting the role that Blatchford (2003: 164) terms 'a guide on the side' rather than the more traditional role of the 'sage on the stage', a theme we develop further in Chapter 10. The teacher was trained as a mathematician and scientist but has found personal satisfaction in attending art classes. She brings this understanding of herself as a learner to this situation and as a result plans and delivers her lesson with the learners' needs to the fore.

---

The lesson starts with an explanation of the structure for the lesson. The teacher has an assistant today; an ICT instructor from a local college is working with one group by using a Swedish multimedia programme. This is to be used for researching the identified topic and for exploring possible forms of presentation.

The teacher sets two Chinese girls, who have recently come to this country and who have very little English, to study some posters of Monet's work and choose the ones they like best. The EAL (English as an additional language) teacher has provided basic word translations to facilitate communication. The two girls settle purposefully to the task.

The teacher then works with one group by explaining that the purpose of the activity is to learn to understand Monet's impressionist style of painting by trying to recreate a section of one of his paintings using his preferred way of working. As she shows how colours are blended on the working surface rather than the palette and how different colours affect adjacent colours by their presence she talks about how she encountered difficulties when she first tried to paint using the impasto technique (for more examples of the value of modelling see Chapter 6). The pupils follow her working practices closely and ask questions which suggest that they are interested in their teacher's skills as much if not more than Monet's. Once the teacher is confident that the pupils are able to proceed she returns to the two Chinese girls, who have chosen their reproductions.

The teacher communicates with these two girls by using cards which contain relevant technical words in Mandarin and English. Apart from this she treats the girls as she treated her first group of pupils. She shows the resources, demonstrates the stages in the process, smiles at her pupils and waits to make certain that they are able to cope. Both girls have well-developed drawing skills. They quickly recognize that they are to use a viewfinder to isolate a section of a Monet painting and draw an enlargement of this using a 1:4 scale. After a very short time the teacher is able to leave the two to work alone while she checks on the ICT group.

The ICT group has been working for 20 minutes. They have clearly benefited from the expertise of their instructor. They talk confidently about the choices they have in accessing Greek music and pictures using websites. Their interests are fully engaged by the information and resources available to them. The pace of working is good. When the teacher arrives she is in the learning mode and the pupils are the instructors. Not all pupils can recall all processes but the instructor and more confident peers intervene and new learning is reinforced (see Chapter 5; concerning the 'dialogic' classroom).

**Plenary**
In constructivist mode the teacher allows the pupils to present and evaluate their work. The group who tackled the painting task found the technique challenging. Their report shows that they have learned a great deal about the underlying difficulties faced when working with wet-on-wet paint as well as the accidental effects which they now recognize add charm to Monet's studies. Their experimental panels offer an opportunity to see what has been achieved as well as what they would now do differently. The ICT group gives a positive account of how helpful the new computer programme could be for topic work. They have already downloaded some information and pictures to support these assertions. The two Chinese girls share the drawings that they have made. They cannot communicate orally but the drawings do so for them. The adults and pupils are captivated by their use of line and space. It is clearly not Monet's, but comes from a different cultural background. The teacher sensitively uses these images to explain cultural differences in the way different peoples portray the world around them. The pupils are still talking about the drawings as they leave the room.

## Formative evaluation

In returning to the questions raised earlier in this chapter, it seems that the Year 6 teacher has a better idea of what her pupils have learned as a result of the experiences offered than the Year 4 teacher does. Her classroom management allowed her to have time to observe and listen to her pupils as well as to learn herself. Her heightened perceptions of their learning occurred in her contact with the ICT group and also in observing her pupils' reactions to the Chinese girls' visual responses to Monet's work. She not only shared learning intentions with her pupils but was also open to their unique contributions as learners. This grew not only from her confidence in delivering the art and design curriculum but also from her awareness of the frustrating and untidy learning process, which is an essential part of the visual arts (see Chapter 5). The Year 4 teacher, on the other hand, had low expectations and was limited in her ability to observe her pupils or talk to them about their understanding because she was largely fielding problems brought about by inadequate tool provision. One boy constructed new knowledge and understanding as a result of the problems he faced and helped others to produce a more successful weft. The majority of pupils had learned the technical words warp and weft, but none of the pupils had learned what an Ikat weaving is or how to make one. If they had listened to the shared learning intention at the start of the lesson many of them might mistakenly believe they had produced one. While the Year 4 teacher operated with behaviourist strategies and her expectations were limited to the notion that learning is, in the main, a response by the learner to the stimuli presented in the lesson, the Year 6 teacher clearly understood that 'human beings do not blindly react to stimuli. They are perceiving, thinking beings with insights, reasoning power, and the ability to make decisions. Humans can and do select the stimuli to which they respond and choose a response that makes sense to them' (Zahorik 1995: 10).

We would also suggest that the Year 6 pupils learned more about another culture from their first-hand experience of the two girls' drawings than the Year 4 pupils did with their wider exposure to different world craft.

## Conclusion

The following passages from *The Arts in Schools* are of interest in considering the kind of educational experience including assessment offered to children.

### Living in the present
To see education only as a preparation for something that happens later risks overlooking the needs and opportunities of the moment. Children do not hatch into adults after a secluded incubation at school. They are living their lives now. Helping them towards an independent and worthwhile life in the adult world of the future presupposes helping them to make sense of and deal with the experiences which they suffer or enjoy in the present. The roles they adopt later and the employment they will seek will partly depend on what they become as individuals – what capacities and capabilities are developed or neglected – during the formative years of education. It follows that schools should enrich and broaden children's experiences through a broad and balanced curriculum. Literacy and numeracy are an important part of education. They should not be mistaken for the whole of it ... Society needs and values more than academic abilities. Children and young people have much more to offer. The arts exemplify some of these other capacities – of intuition, creativity, sensibility and practical skills. We maintain that an education in these is quite as important for all children as an education

of the more academic kind and that not to have this is to stunt and distort growth as intelligent, feeling and capable individuals.

(Calouste Gulbenkian Foundation 1982: 1)

Tyler (1949: 1) raised four relevant questions about the educational experiences schools provide. They are:

1   What educational purposes should the school seek to attain?
2   What educational experiences can be provided that are likely to attain these purposes?
3   How can these educational experiences be effectively organized?
4   How can we determine whether these purposes are being attained?

Many education theorists agree that it is essential to teach with an end in mind – that is, to define an objective, a learning intention, the quality aimed for. The instruction should be designed so that the pupil will reach that end, will construct that knowledge or gain proficiency in that skill. The manner of assessment – how the teacher identifies pupils' competence – can consist of direct interaction (conversations, open-ended questions and answers) or indirect interaction (testing). This is a highly useful way of thinking about instruction, but this approach has its limitations and, it may be argued, should not be used exclusively. In the visual arts, open-ended exploration and experimentation or true creativity are valid ends in themselves. This constructivist view of teaching has implications for how assessment is viewed.

If the real goal for pupils is the search for meaning and the construction of knowledge the teacher is not afraid to ask questions to which they may not already know the answer. The teacher asks questions to involve pupils in creating meaning for themselves and in so doing learning how to learn. As Maxine Greene (1994: 398) writes:

> I would like to see students and their teachers to become conscious of the need for transformative, risk-taking, higher-order thinking ... I want to see people resonate to the kind of knowing that plunges them deeply to central ideas and complex understandings; I want them to feel connections between what they are coming to know and the contexts of their lives or their lived worlds. I want to provoke dialogue and eager transactions in the classroom, whether they have to do with works of art or with art-making and perceiving.

How, we wonder, would the average primary school teacher react if a pupil exhibited the qualities referred to above and was confident enough to challenge the grading of their creative work, without any explanation of the criteria used or the qualities aimed for, as in the example which follows?

A 'C'. I got a 'C' for my coat-hanger sculpture!! How can you get a 'C' on a coat-hanger sculpture? May I ask a question? Was I judged on the sculpture itself or was I judged on my talent over which I have no control? If I was judged on my effort I was judged unfairly because I tried as hard as I could. Was I judged on my learning about this project? If so, are you my teacher also being judged on your ability to transmit knowledge? Are you willing to share my 'C'?

Research shows that grading has little meaning for pupils and labelling can be destructive for future learning (see Chapter 5). Surely one of the crucial questions for anyone trying to develop constructivist assessment practices in the expressive arts in 2004 is:

- How do you strike a balance between the need to define clear learning objectives in advance of instruction and the need for learning intentions to emerge as a result of constructing new knowledge, understanding and skill development?

It is not easy for a teacher to step back from a directoral role to a facilitative one, particularly in the present climate of accountability and league tables, but it is worth trying.

One way to achieve this balance in Key Stage 2 (Years 3–6) is to help the pupils develop sketchbooks as think books. In this way they not only respond to learning intentions specified by the teacher but also generate learning goals which are more specific to themselves. For some pupils – for example, with a high degree of visual/spatial intelligence – well-drawn images or clearly defined visual models may be worthwhile goals, whereas for those pupils with a strong verbal/linguistic intelligence the key may be constructing art knowledge by reading and making annotated notes. If pupil-generated learning intentions were acceptable in this way, teachers might gain a clearer understanding of pupils' perceptions. If sketchbook work is dated regularly it gives the teacher and the pupil an idea of progression or regression over time, and opens up a real opportunity for talking meaningfully about the work.

Teachers do talk to individuals regularly, but as one Year 4 girl in the case study reported in Chapters 3 and 4 commented, 'I don't think she [teacher] has ever talked to me personally' (as opposed to about her work). Creativity is often an intuitive process and cannot be explained simply. Ross *et al.* (1993) carried out research into the use of assessment conversations in the expressive arts. They found that learners have to have time to recover what they have done before they can evaluate how well they have done. They also found that teachers had to be quite knowledgeable about the domain being talked about in order to facilitate this process. The examples of classroom practice used in this chapter confirm these findings.

# 10 Formative Assessment and History

## Introduction

We begin this chapter with a brief overview of orientations to history. This is important since one's sense of what history is for has implications for what and how one assesses pupil achievement in it. We then go on to discuss some principles of effective history teaching and assessment, drawing on the Nuffield Primary History Project (NPHP) and on *History in the National Curriculum (HNC)* (DfE 1995). We then discuss ways of fostering self- and peer assessment in history. The final section revisits a theme we introduced in the first chapter – recognizing what is significant in formative assessment. In doing this we consider children's understanding of chronology and how this can be promoted and assessed through story, thus integrating history and English.

## Orientations to history and assessment implications

Why teach history? What history ought to be taught and how should it be approached? These are questions about values and it is likely that they will remain matters of debate (even heated debate) among historians, history teachers, curriculum designers and policy makers. We will overview some history perspectives briefly here, although we do not claim to address underlying complexities.

One perspective shared by some child developmentalists is that young children are not developmentally ready to tackle the complexities of historical study. Children are assumed to have difficulty grasping 'pastness' and are assumed to benefit from a curriculum that begins with themselves, their own families, school, and gradually moves to communities (see Brophy and Van-Sledright 1997; Bage 2000 for a full discussion of these perspectives). Another perspective argues that history is primarily about citizenship education and that its major purpose is the promotion of commitment to the public good, and active participation in the nation's democratic processes through decision making and problem solving experiences. As John Fines (1994: 28) said in a discussion paper about progression in history: 'there is not some simple ladder of goals, targets, achievements ... but everybody is in the business of learning to work in the history way, which we know will do them good, preparing good, self confident and well prepared citizens of the future rather than just more historians'. The aim of participatory democracy is privileged over maintaining history's disciplinary integrity, so integration is often favoured over separate subject teaching. Those who favour an emphasis on subject matter, on the other hand, push for 'disciplinary history' (Hirsch 1987). This perspective advocates that children begin history early in their schooling with historical myths and stories followed by a more rigorous chronological study of history in remaining primary classes. *HNC* is arguably a mix of the latter two.

Several studies of children's historical understanding which were conducted over the past two decades or so (e.g. Dickinson and Lee 1984; Sansom 1987; Hallden 1994; Lee *et al.* 1996) have shown that young children can manage historical thinking, can empathize with people from the past and indeed are capable of meaningful historical understanding much earlier than previously had been assumed. The work of Lee, in particular, has been important in showing that historical imagination and empathy are necessary features of historical understanding; that these develop gradually, that they can be fostered by teaching, and, more specifically, that they can be promoted by discussion, questioning, attending to pupils' prior knowledge of other historical contexts and by linking the period under study to pupils' own lives (Brophy and VanSledright 1997). All this fits well with what we have already discussed in Chapter 1 about learning more generally.

In a study of the practice of junior school history, focusing on teachers nominated as effective, Peter Knight (1991) identified two pedagogical approaches to history – one he termed 'history teaching as exposure' and he contrasts this with the objectives-led structure of the National Curriculum. On the basis of his evidence, teachers' beliefs and practices were more orientated to the 'exposure' model than to the objectives one. Teachers appeared to be more interested in their pupils' motivation and engagement in the historical topics on offer than in chasing after precise learning outcomes.

Although the National Curriculum was in its infancy when this study was conducted and we acknowledge that practice has most likely changed since, the implications for assessment of the 'exposure' perspective are interesting and it is likely that they still resonate with many primary teachers. The fact that history has not been subjected to the demands of summative assessment that have afflicted the core areas adds weight to the likelihood that the exposure model still provides a valid account of practice. The point is that if, as Knight notes, history is seen as a matter of exposing children to the subject, then differentiation by task, criterion-referenced assessment, recaps and summaries at the beginning and end of lessons are all rather unnecessary. Moreover, progression is not an issue and topics may be selected for their interest and potential to engage and motivate, rather than to promote key historical skills or understanding.

At another level, bearing in mind the argument we make in Chapter 1 about communities of practice, what is important is that teachers in any given school need to share a philosophy of history teaching in order to agree on the criteria by which they judge success in history. As we have argued throughout this book, what counts as success has to be communicated and shared with the pupils themselves so they know what they know and know what to do to make further progress. Knight found that his teachers' ideas about progression were vague in so far as they did not refer to criteria to differentiate between the work of lower and upper juniors. The differences that were discerned in what the teachers recommended for lower and upper juniors were about differences in the materials and the activities they saw as appropriate, rather than differences in expected achievements. Teachers did not articulate outcomes and Knight interpreted this as signalling a problem for progression. The teachers reported that they would teach in much the same way regardless of the class taught. The vast majority of the teachers in the study said that they set similar tasks for all of the children, expecting them to engage with the tasks at their own level (differentiation by outcome).

It seems that what teachers said about assessment was equally vague. Knight (1991: 78) concluded that:

> As for assessing what children had learned, it was clear that this rarely, if ever, took the form of assessing learning against criteria

which were sensitive to levels of understanding of chronology, empathy, or evidence handling. The methods of assessment which they described were intuitive, unfocused and relaxed – assessment of children's levels of engagement as much as assessment of learning outcomes.

Later in the study he notes that 'Strikingly absent is evidence of children's progress in learning and evidence of what children had learnt. Engagement, not learning outcomes, dominated teacher thinking' (p. 80).

*HNC* expects teachers to promote engagement *and* specific learning outcomes. We now consider some of the principles and procedures of effective history teaching, bearing in mind the demands of *HNC*.

## Effective teaching and assessment in history: *HNC* and the NPHP

In the mid-1990s the NPHP team worked in schools supporting the teaching of all the history study units for Key Stages 1 and 2. The overarching principle guiding the project was that children should be involved in 'doing history'. The kernel of this is that whatever the age of the child or the class, history in schools should parallel the thinking involved when historians do history. Five principles that guide the NPHP approach are (Verrier 1997: 1):

1   Questioning: history is about asking and answering questions, enquiring and investigating.
2   Challenges: questioning challenges children to make connections between events and periods, to debate issues and to investigate further.
3   Integrity and economy of sources: real history is taught through authentic sources of history. More wide-ranging and useful questions can be asked of a few well-chosen sources than of an unfocused jumble.
4   Depth: genuine historical knowledge demands study in depth to develop expertise and confidence.
5   Accessibility: we make history accessible to all children by starting with what the children can do and building on that, using a variety of teaching approaches, going at the right pace for all the children's understanding, using whole-class teaching and debate, and co-operative pair and group work.

*HNC* identifies several areas, in its key elements, that teachers need to assess in history. Taken together these provide a profile of historical learning.

These then constitute aspects that are important for formative assessment in history. Table 10.1 details the expectations in history for each of the key elements.

However, several researchers have identified deficiencies in the assessment criteria for *HNC*. For instance, Jon Nichol and Jacqueline Dean (1997: 130), on the basis of their Nuffield-funded research and development work, make a cogent case for three common criteria that they believe enable teachers to assess all aspects of the key elements. These are *coherence, sophistication* and *depth of knowledge*. Coherence, they suggest, can be considered on a continuum, at one end of which may lie a set of unrelated statements while the other end may contain an explanation that is plausible and that pulls together different strands of evidence to form an integrated account with contradictions explained. Sophistication, they suggest, involves the learner's ability to deal with complexity, to take account of different perspectives and to offer interpretations based on historical evidence. Depth of knowledge bears on the extent and variety of knowledge that the pupil shows in historical work. It develops, they suggest, through attending to a number of historical events and examining them comprehensively. Such attention, it is assumed, leads to a sense of period.

As in other domains discussed in this book, assessment tasks in the domain of history need to align with tasks normally set to promote learning. They also need to be based on different methods, from drama and role-play to writing, and from art to oral expression. Opportunities like role-play have tremendous potential for fostering and displaying learning; role-play and other dramatic approaches have the potential to engage learners very directly – emotionally and bodily, as well as intellectually and analytically – and by so doing to enhance the quality and complexity of their thinking.

We have chosen the next example because it involves group work. Blatchford *et al.* (2001: 164) have argued that groups within the class should be considered not just in terms of increasing teacher attention to pupils, but in terms of taking seriously pupil self-directed group work in classes. A teacher need not be a 'sage on the stage' at all times, they suggest. Even in smaller classes the teacher can afford to be a 'guide on the side'. The example below requires pupils to use their imagination as well as their cognitive skills and it has the potential to integrate assessment with teaching and learning. It is taken from Nichol and Dean's (1997: 135–6) work with teachers.

**Table 10.1** Expectations in history

| Key elements | By end of Year 2 | By end of Year 4 | By end of Year 6 |
|---|---|---|---|
| Chronology | Use terms concerned with the passing of time, such as *then, now, in the past* | Recognize that the past can be divided into periods of time such as Tudor, Victorian | Make appropriate use of dates and chronological conventions such as BC, AD, century and decade |
| Range and depth of historical knowledge and understanding | Demonstrate factual knowledge and understanding of aspects of the past beyond living memory and of some of the main events and people studied | Demonstrate factual knowledge and understanding of some of the main events and people covered in the study units | Demonstrate factual knowledge and understanding of aspects of Britain and other countries drawn from the Key Stage 2 programme of study. Describe some of the main events, people and changes studied |
| | Make distinctions between aspects of their own times and past times | Recognize some of the similarities and differences between periods | Use this factual knowledge and understanding to describe characteristic features of past societies and periods and identify changes within and across periods |
| | Begin to recognize that there are reasons why people in the past acted in the ways that they did | Begin to give reasons for, and results of, the main events and changes studied, and why people in the past acted as they did | Give some reasons for, and results of, the main events and changes studied, and why people in the past acted as they did |
| Interpretations of history | Begin to identify some ways in which the past is represented | Identify with confidence some of the different ways in which the past is represented | Show how some aspects of the past have been represented and interpreted in different ways |

**Table 10.1** (*continued*)

| | | |
|---|---|---|
| Historical enquiry | Answer, through simple observation, questions about the past by using sources of information | Ask and answer questions about the past by using sources of information in a variety of ways | Select and combine information from more than one source of information to find out about aspects of the periods studied |
| Organization and communication | Convey an awareness and understanding of the past in a variety of ways – written, oral and pictorial | Present recalled or selected information, using specialist terms in ways which show understanding | Produce work, organized and structured appropriately for the purpose |

*Source:* DfE (1995)

| Acts to save your head |
| --- |

The Viking topic was in its fourth week. In earlier weeks the pupils had dug a Viking burial mound; they had established, through placename study, the pattern of Viking settlement in Yorkshire; they had studied different facets of Viking life. The pupils were invited into the past by the teachers telling them the story from Egil's saga of how Egil was captured by his bitter enemy Eirik Bloodaxe, King of Yorvik (York) and was about to be killed. However, his friend Arinbjorn – one of Bloodaxe's henchmen – persuaded his captors to give Egil one night's grace before bringing him before Bloodaxe. Egil had only one night to think of a means of saving himself. Here the storytelling stopped and the pupils were grouped in threes and were asked to take the role of Egil and come up with a convincing plea to save themselves. They had 15 minutes to prepare during which time the teachers rearranged the classroom to look like Bloodaxe's great hall. Then each Egil group walked up the great hall, knelt to Bloodaxe and his wife Gunnhild (the teachers) and made their bids for their life. Here is what the ten groups of three did:

1   A fake conversion to Christianity: this group came forward bearing a cross and intoning Christian prayers for forgiveness.
2   Bribery, with offers of jewels and silver in return for life.
3   Bribery again but more strategic, saying, 'If you spare my head, I will give you half my land and all my belongings when I die naturally.'
4–5 Pleas for forgiveness, appealing to the king and queen's better natures.
6–8 Poems, one appealing to the pair's past friendship, another praising the queen (Oh Queen/you are/such a/delight/You make/the whole kingdom/come to light).
9   A combination of the above: 'Would you like cargo with jewels and gold? And maybe we could give you some of our land in Iceland. And maybe my lord might be interested in some stories for when you drink and talk with your men.'
10  An offer of single combat, and when this was scornfully refused by Bloodaxe, an astute second offer: to kill King Athelstan of England (who trusted Egil) and make Bloodaxe king of all England in Athelstan.

*Source*: Nichol and Dean (1997: 135–6)

How might one interpret these pupils' historical understanding? Using the criteria noted above, what might one say about their ability to produce a coherent account of the past, their demonstration of the complexity of the historical situation and the depth of their knowledge about the period? Taking account of these criteria, Nichol and Dean argue that the strategies above vary considerably. At one end of the (sophistication) spectrum they note the rather naive and unlikely strategies of groups 4 and 5 and at the other end the highly plausible and politically astute approach of groups 1 and 10.

As required by *HNC*, groups 1 and 10 both show historical knowledge and understanding – group 1 that the Viking period featured conversions to Christianity and group 10 showing knowledge of the political power context in England at the time. However, as these authors point out, group 1's strategy, although coherent and sophisticated, lacks the plausibility evident in group 10's approach. The approach of the latter is more credible in the context of the Viking period in that it had a stronger sense of the size of the bribe that would be needed; it shows a more nuanced grasp of power struggles and structures. As the authors put it, 'on the coherence, sophistication, depth ladder group 10 is several rungs higher than group 1' (Nichol and Dean 1997: 136). In their view this flags up the limitations of the assessment model within the National Curriculum.

## Knowing how your work is judged: self- and peer assessment again

A point that we would want to emphasize here is that unless teachers engage their pupils in conversations about the coherence, sophistication and depth of knowledge of their accounts – whether oral, written or dramatized, as in the example here – many pupils are likely to continue exhibiting the level of understanding of groups 4 and 5 above. They may remain naive for longer since they may be unaware of possible ways of thinking about acting. They need opportunities to discuss the merits and demerits of these strategies in terms of the success criteria of coherence, sophistication and depth of knowledge. Pupils are likely to need lots of opportunities to talk about what counts as a good historical account in the context of several examples of their own and others' work. In this regard self- and peer assessment, as we discussed more fully in Chapter 5, are important.

Almost a decade ago, John Fines (1994: 28) noted that 'When children know what we are after from them, then they will try to give it. When they do not, it is all a shot in the dark'. Helping them know what counts as quality work has to be ongoing. The teacher can help learners understand how their work is judged in history by equipping them with a language (or a metalanguage) to describe their own achievements and learning. This could be developed by giving specific and task-orientated feedback on their own work (see Bage 2000). Drawing on Bage (2000), the teacher's response with Key Stage 1 pupils might include such statements as:

- *I can see that you can categorize toys (clothes, forms of transport, weapons etc.) into 'then' and 'now'.*
- *You are able to place these objects (e.g. different clothes) on the class timeline.*
- *I can see that you can distinguish between the past and the present in your own life and in the lives of others.*
- *You are able to sequence historical events and objects.*
- *You are able to retell stories about the past.*
- *You are able to find information to answer questions about the past.*
- *You understand lots of reasons why people in the past acted as they did.*
- *You know some of the ways in which the past is represented.*

Pupils can also be encouraged to describe themselves in terms of what they have achieved or say what a piece of work tells about their learning. For example, the following statements might be appropriate for those in upper primary classes:

- *I can describe events, peoples and changes and use that knowledge to offer reasons and results.*
- *I can place key buildings on the class timeline (e.g. the ruins of an abbey, the local school, a Viking longboat etc.).*
- *I understand that some events (giving examples), people and changes have been interpreted differently and I can suggest some reasons why.*
- *I can understand and use specialist historical vocabulary like invasion, evidence, rebellion, treaty, slavery etc.*
- *I can locate sources and use them to assemble information and I can evaluate that information.*
- *I can link different sources of information about a period in history and write an account of that period; I can devise my own questions and answer them using different sources.*
- *I can produce structured accounts using dates and historical terms.*

Pupils might also be encouraged to include reference to the 'next steps' for their historical learning as they describe their learning – for example, *'I understand important events* [perhaps be more specific and identify those events], *peoples and changes. I now need to learn how that/some event(s), people and changes have been interpreted differently by different people'.*

One particularly successful question-generating strategy, developed by Ogle (1986), is the K-W-L strategy or Know, Want-to-Know, Learned. It can be used with the whole class, small groups or by a single individual. Before a historical source (or indeed any non-fiction) text is read, the pupils brainstorm all they know abut the topic and list the results as bullet points in a table that is ruled into three column headings as follows:

| What we know | What we want to know | What we learned |
|---|---|---|
|  |  |  |

The first column is about activating prior knowledge concerning the historical period or event. Under the second column the pupils generate some questions they think the source or document might address. This part requires them to think about questions, to predict and to reflect on the information that is needed. Following their study of the document (either silently or as a shared activity) they summarize, using bullet points again, the main points they have learned. Here they have to reflect, consolidate, evaluate and summarize. A fourth column could be added requesting pupils to record how they felt about the material in the text and how they plan to use the information they have learned.

A similar strategy to the above is described by Nichol and Dean (1997: 127) which involves supplying pupils with starter and summarizing questions and statements such as the following:

- *I have used these sources . . .*
- *From them I learned that . . .*
- *I believe my account/conclusion is right because . . .*

Or:

- *I have found out that . . .*
- *How I know is/the evidence for my conclusion is . . .*

A checklist that pupils might be occasionally encouraged to use as they carry out a historical task might include the following questions that they can ask themselves:

- *Have I understood what I have to do?*
- *What sources of information have I used?*
- *How reliable are my sources?*
- *Have I checked my evidence against other sources?*
- *What is the most likely explanation, taking all the evidence into account?*

Pupils' learning is accelerated when they have frameworks or models to help them to understand what it is they know and need to know and to reflect on what they have learned and how they have learned. The above strategies are intended to provide that kind of supporting framework or scaffolding.

Like any subject, what is important in assessment for learning history is not comparisons between learners or between schools but an understanding of what counts as doing history and then assessment against one's own performance last time. Fines (1994: 28) puts this complex point simply: 'Now we know what doing history means, can we say that this piece of work is any better or worse than what you produced last time?'

## Recognizing the significance of what learners say

In Chapter 1 we made the point that, while observation is a vital means of obtaining assessment information about pupils, recognizing what is significant is far from a simple matter. This depends on who is doing the looking or more particularly on the ability of the observer to notice what is really significant about the evidence (what learners say, do and write). This demands what is known as 'pedagogical content knowledge'. In other words, if teachers understand the internal architecture of the topic being taught (content) and have the teaching skills to listen to pupils and to probe their reasoning, taking their responses on board (pedagogy), then they are likely to pick up on what is insightful evidence about their learners' developing understanding. As a result the teacher is likely to be in a better position to intervene effectively.

In this final section of the chapter we will explore children's understanding of time and more particularly how teachers might recognize what is significant about that understanding. Chronology is fundamental to historical understanding, and unsurprisingly it features highly in the programmes of study and in the assessment statements of *HNC*. One way to develop and assess children's awareness of time is through narrative fiction. Since narrative is a fundamental means of understanding and interpreting experience, it is no surprise that children learn about chronology through the manipulations of time that characterize much narrative. Stories require children to impose structure, to sequence events and to make connections between causes and effects – some of the basic requirements of historical understanding.

But what do we mean by chronology or time here? What kind of 'time' concepts should we promote in learners? How do we recognize what concepts of time are present or lacking in our pupils? In a fascinating study of young children (3–9 years), Patricia Hoodless (2002) established that through the use of story, children can show that they have developed quite complex concepts of time – manipulated time, dream time, parallel time and the notion of time as subjective (that time as a personal experience can differ from real forms of measurement). She assessed this understanding through the use of storybooks. Very young children were able to use the vocabulary of time and chronology, including words for placing events in time (e.g. 'then', 'now', 'before' etc.). And they could use this vocabulary in reasoning and justifying responses.

The sequencing of events – a skill fundamental to understanding more complex chronological sequencing – is the most obvious aspect of time that an assessment of chronology might involve. Hoodless assessed learners' understanding of time through the use of two particular picture books: *Come Away from the Water, Shirley* (Burningham 1977) and *Where the Wild Things Are* (Sendak 1988) – two stories that manipulate time in various ways, both using parallel times and unreal or imaginary time. On the grounds that fiction provides a good vehicle for encouraging pupils to talk, explore and extend understanding as well as a means of (developing) and assessing their awareness of chronology, Hoodless used a range of questioning techniques to probe their understanding.

She found that young learners were, to varying degrees, aware of jumps in time, they were aware of the omission of a period of time in a story, they were aware of flashbacks and flash-forwards. They were also aware of parallel time or the notion of different events occurring simultaneously. With reference to this awareness of a range of concepts of time, she says, 'these digressions from simple chronology' provide evidence of a child's 'awareness of sequence, of particular relevance to the use of time lines and the placing of events in time where skill in moving back and forth in time is a prerequisite'. She adds, 'An understanding of parallel times is particularly important for a child learning to place contemporaneous events appropriately in time' (2002: 186).

Here are two examples from the study (2002: 194) and from the use of the two stories, which demonstrate children's awareness of parallel time; but also of note is the assessor's style of interaction.

*Where the Wild Things Are*
PH: Why was his supper still hot when he got back?
*Child 1*: Because it was only a dream and he hadn't gone for a year away.
*Child 2*: I think that because his breakfast was still hot; I think it was because it was a dream; he was dreaming.
*Child 3*: His mother came up somewhere in the middle of the dream or somewhere at the end.

*Come Away from the Water, Shirley*
PH: What do you think was happening in that story?
*Child 1*: Shirely wasn't listening to what her mum and dad were saying ... because she was on the pirate ship and she was sailing away, and she [her mother] thought she was throwing stones and bringing seaweed back with her.
*Child 2*: I know, she was listening to no one and she kept on ... Shirley, would you like a drink?

Since the children in the transcript here were able to take on board the simultaneous experiences of the two characters and their respective mothers, Hoodless concludes that they were aware of the notion of time as contemporaneous or parallel time – a feature previous research has shown to be important in developing chronological understanding.

However, we are not suggesting that the above approach – the use of suitable fiction – can on its own develop and assess the chronological understanding necessary for historical knowledge, skill and understanding. What we are emphasizing though is the need to attend and listen to what learners say in answer to open-ended questions. Bage (2000: 93) provides excellent guidance on how to develop all aspects of history within *HNC*. Some of the questions about chronology can be used both to develop and to assess learners' understanding. Such questions are likely to elicit extended, thoughtful responses that would provide insights into pupils' understandings and misunderstandings:

- How can we tell which of these objects might have been used a long time ago?
- Can we put these pictures or objects in order and explain our choice, with the oldest first and the most recent last (e.g. relating to transport, buildings, armour, costume)?
- Which of these things might your grandparents have used? Explain your choice.
- Read the story. What changes happened to the characters during the time of the story?
- What does this (artefact, book, picture etc.) tell us about (cooking, transport, entertainment etc.) when your grandparents were young?
- How could we find out about how life has changed in (schools, villages, factories, etc.) over the past (50, 1000, 100) years?
- Referring to pictures of place, how can we tell at what time in history this picture might have been taken?
- What are the newest/oldest things we can see?
- What might have been there then that has disappeared now?

We would highlight several issues about the above approaches. First, that the use of suitable fiction (stories that manipulate chronology) provided a context that enabled the pupils to show their understanding. In Chapter 1 we noted that tasks that are concrete and within the experience of the individual allow the pupil to show what they know or can do. The use of story here fulfilled this criterion. Second, the style of interaction, where the researcher posed open-ended questions and responded to the pupils' responses, allowed pupils themselves to offer a range of responses. The value of such interaction, as we noted in Chapter 1 and explored more fully in Chapter 5 (see p. 60–62), lies in its ability to allow the teacher to get into the child's thinking and reasoning. Third, the fiction example shows how concepts of time can be developed and assessed effectively through history and English. Given the pressure on curriculum time of an overloaded curriculum that is defined in terms of traditional subjects, the opportunity to integrate subject areas is itself of value. Finally, it showed how the complexity of the concept being assessed needs to be grasped by the assessor. Without an understanding of the subtleties of the concept of time being assessed, the teacher is likely to miss crucial evidence, to not recognize what might be significant.

## Conclusion

This chapter shows that how and what we assess is bound up with our definitions of the subject in question. What we assess in history cannot be separated from what we think history is and what aspects of it are important. Recognizing what is significant historical understanding and feeding this back to learners in a way that makes sense to them are key elements of effective history assessment.

# 11 Assessing What We Value: Learning Dispositions in the Early Years

## Introduction

Our nets define what we shall catch says Elliot Eisner (1985), referring to the fact that what we assess is what we get, and that we value what we assess. How helpful are our current assessment policies for promoting the learning that we value most? Although we discussed official policy on assessment in Chapter 2, we did not attend exclusively to the early years of school. Here (and in the next chapter) we examine assessment for learning with more specific reference to the early years of a child's schooling.

The neuropsychologist Paul Broks (2003) says that the human being is a storytelling machine and that the self is a story. Much of the thinking about assessment in this chapter and in the next is captured in that idea of the self as a story.

In this chapter we consider the Foundation Stage Profile (FSP) and what it may offer in terms of useful information for teaching and learning. Then we consider aspects of learning that up to now have typically neither been explicitly promoted nor assessed – what some have termed 'learning dispositions' or habits of mind. We explore what these dispositions are and why they are important. The next chapter will extend the ideas introduced here.

## The FSP: assessing what we really value?

First, we chart briefly the shift from baseline assessment to the FSP. Statutory baseline assessment was introduced in September 1998, and meant that primary schools were required to assess children on entry to school using an accredited baseline assessment scheme. Some 90 schemes were accredited – all based on the Desirable Learning Outcomes that were the goals for children in the term after their fifth birthday. Schools were then required to submit their results to their LEA who would in turn pass the results on to the QCA. In September 2000 the Foundation Stage was introduced, which means that children in early years settings, including reception classes in schools, are working towards the Early Learning Goals (ELGs) and the curriculum provision in the settings is informed by the QCA's guidance for this stage. The ELGs are the attainments expected for children at the end of the Foundation Stage as they enter Key Stage 1 (see QCA 2003). In effect this means that the accredited schemes for baseline assessment have been rendered obsolete since they do not conform to these learning goals. New arrangements were piloted in July 2002 and became statutory in the school year 2002/3.

The FSP is the new statutory assessment for children in the final year of the Foundation Stage. It replaces baseline assessment and the first profiles are due to be completed at the end of the summer term in 2003 (as we complete this book). The QCA say they have chosen the word 'profile' carefully, claiming that it reflects 'a new approach to assessment'. The QCA website states: 'The Foundation Stage Profile is a picture of what a child has achieved, knows and can do. It is based on the early learning goals and the *Curriculum Guidance for the Foundation Stage*. There are no tests. There are no tasks. You build the profile over the year'. It goes on to emphasize that the FSP is about assessment for learning and that the *Curriculum* and the *Profile* together are intended to support early years staff in providing a broad, motivating curriculum linked to the ELGs.

The curriculum at the Foundation Stage is designed to promote the following areas:

- personal, social and emotional development;
- communication, language and literacy;
- mathematical development;

- knowledge and understanding of the world;
- physical development;
- creative development.

The FSP is based on practitioners' ongoing observations and assessments over all these six areas of learning (outlined in *Curriculum Guidance for the Foundation Stage*: QCA/DfEE 2000). The FSP is described by the QCA as 'a way of summing up each child's progress and learning needs at the end of the Foundation Stage'. For the typical child this will be at the end of the reception year in primary school. The FSP consists of 13 assessment scales with nine points on each scale. There are three scales associated with personal, social and emotional development, namely 'dispositions and attitudes', 'social development' and 'emotional development'. There are four scales associated with communication, language and literacy, namely 'language for communication and thinking', 'linking with sounds and letters', 'reading' and 'writing'. There are three scales associated with mathematical development, namely 'numbers as labels and counting', 'calculating' and 'shape, space and measures'. There are three further scales, each one associated with each of the remaining three curriculum areas listed above.

The *Foundation Stage Profile Handbook* (QCA 2003) presents the nine points of each scale, and below each point on the scale is further elaboration and exemplification, demonstrating the kinds of behaviour and contexts that could count as evidence of a child's achievement. Some of this exemplification is drawn from *Curriculum Guidance for the Foundation Stage*. Table 11.1 reproduces the scale for 'dispositions and attitudes' together with elaboration offered by the QCA. We return to dispositions themselves later in the chapter (and in the next one) but for now we present Table 11.1 as an illustration of the scales that teachers are required to use. The first three points of each scale describe development that has not yet reached the level of the ELG, points 4 to 8 describe the level of the ELG and are non-hierarchical. Point 9 describes development beyond the level of the ELG. Practitioners have to judge whether each scale point has been attained by recording 'yes' or 'no' for each point for each child. Point 9 can only be awarded if points 1–8 have been achieved.

On the grounds that what we assess is what we really value, it is worth noting the status attributed to literacy and numeracy here. Five of the thirteen scales describe attainment in these areas. By comparison, just one scale is devoted to describing the young learner's dispositions and attitudes to learning, although there is some overlap in the social and emotional scales. Whether we have got the nets right (following Eisner) is a debatable point here. In this regard we think it is important to highlight two issues. The first thing to say is that the FSP is, in our view, a significant improvement on the form of baseline assessment that preceded it. It draws practitioners' attention

**Table 11.1** Scale for personal, social and emotional development

| Scale point | Elaboration |
| --- | --- |
| 1 Shows an interest in classroom activities through observation or participation | The child shows curiosity, displaying a brief interest in activities, by watching or listening for a short time or by joining in, sometimes with adult support |
| 2 Dresses, undresses and manages own personal hygiene with adult support | With some support, the child is able to dress and undress for outdoor or play activities |
| 3 Displays high levels of involvement in self-chosen activities | Through a widening range of activities, the child shows high levels of involvement, for example becoming involved in a self-chosen activity, which they persevere to complete. If interrupted, they would be keen to return to the activity |
| 4 Dresses and undresses independently and manages own personal hygiene | The child shows personal independence, putting on outdoor clothes, washing hands or pouring out drinks at snack time |
| 5 Selects and uses activities and resources independently | When taking part in self-initiated or adult-initiated activities, the child selects resources from the range provided and can add to these by choosing from other resources which are accessible. The child selects activities independently from a range provided or from other appropriate activities that are accessible |
| 6 Continues to be interested, motivated and excited to learn | The child engages in a range of activities, they display motivation to learn, through attentiveness and perseverance. They may show excitement when anticipating and participating in some of these |
| 7 Is confident to try new activities, initiate ideas and speak in a familiar group | When new classroom activities are introduced, the child is confident to try them. They initiate ideas, either by trying things out individually or by making suggestions when working in a small group. The child speaks confidently in a familiar group, for example asking and answering questions during book-sharing sessions or describing some of their experiences to other children. This may be demonstrated in small groups, for example the child describing to the group a model they have made in a construction activity, or in larger group situations such as circle time |
| 8 Maintains attention and concentrates | The child is attentive and able to concentrate well, for example listening attentively while the practitioner describes the range of interesting activities on offer or reads a story aloud |

**Table 11.1**  (*continued*)

| Scale point | Elaboration |
| --- | --- |
| 9 Sustains involvement and perseveres, particularly when trying to solve a problem or reach a satisfactory conclusion | When taking part in a range of challenging activities, the child sustains very high levels of involvement, often showing reluctance to leave an activity until reaching an outcome which they consider satisfactory. The challenging activities include some instigated by the practitioner as well as those initiated by the child |

*Source*: QCA (2003)

to important aspects of the young person's learning, not least dispositions and attitudes. It offers a more holistic approach to assessment in so far as it is not based exclusively on what might be termed 'academic' subject areas. More specifically, it acknowledges the importance of children being interested in learning and motivated to learn – it is not merely focused on attainment. In this sense it focuses the practitioner on learning and on the processes of learning. References in the *Handbook* (QCA 2003) also suggest that parents, carers and educators are involved in the process. All of this is a major improvement over what operated in the recent past.

Our second point concerns some difficulties. Despite the proclaimed emphasis on assessment for learning, there remains a tension between summative and formative purposes. The 'tick sheet' (yes/no) approach, designed to fulfil summative purposes and to be manageable, may hinder the production of a 'rich respectful account' (Drummond 1999: 34) of a child's learning. It may push practitioners more towards 'assessing for convergence' rather than divergence, where the emphasis will be on sameness rather than diversity and children as free spirits (Drummond 1999).

Although the many examples offered by the QCA in their guidance notes are useful in demonstrating the kinds of behaviour and contexts that could count as evidence of a child's achievement, they lack the kind of detail that would indicate continuity and progression, and they are thin on contextual background. The point we made above about the strong emphasis on literacy and numeracy in the FSP more than hints at a desire to link assessment at the Foundation Stage with SATs at Key Stage 1. What the consequences of the assessments at the Foundation Stage will be remain to be seen. As we have argued already, the use to which assessment information is put for the benefit of learners is what is really crucial and it is too early to say what those consequences will be in relation to the FSP.

We recognize and welcome, however, the greater emphasis on learning dispositions and we elaborate on this theme in a moment. The context in which learning and assessment happens we believe merits greater recognition and we develop our argument for this case both here and in the next chapter as we elaborate on some of the ways learning dispositions might be promoted and assessed.

## Learning dispositions

We begin this section with some brief scenarios of two pairs of children, the first one witnessed by the first author recently, the second drawn from the literature. The features of learning underlying these scenarios are discussed in the work of Carr (1999, 2001), Carr and Claxton (2002), Claxton (1999), Dweck and Leggett (1988), Krechersky (1991) and Wigfield *et al.* (1998).

---

**Molly and Sinéad**

Both are almost 3 years' old. They are cousins who, with their mothers and their Aunt Helen, have just arrived at a deserted seaside which is a few miles away from where they live. It is a warm, sunny day in autumn and the tide is coming in. Katie runs down over the stones to get onto the sand and nearer the water. She glances back once to check that her mother is approving and then shouts at Fiona to come on. Fiona, however, is clinging to her mother and observes her cousin from a safe distance. Her mother and Helen encourage her to follow Katie; she doesn't and continues to cling to her mother's leg. Helen walks down the stones after Katie and they both play running against the tide. Occasionally Katie checks that her mother is not far away, that she is in fact watching and enjoying what she sees; several times Katie beckons and shouts at Fiona to join in. But Fiona resists. Later Katie wants to walk along the high wall around the beach. She runs off, climbs up unaided from the beach side and looks down at the other side which, she now discovers, has a drop of several feet. Thinking that this may not be safe and that her mother would not approve, she looks in her direction. Her mother is shouting at her not to walk on the wall; she obeys and waits for her mother to come over and take her down. Fiona has burst into tears and is being comforted by her mother. Much later, when it's almost time to go home, Fiona is walking along the stones towards the waves, holding her mother's hand. These responses are typical of the children.

**Izzah and Nathan**

Izzah and Nathan are friends. They are both 7 years' old and are in the same class in school. They are both high achievers and do well in all subjects, especially mathematics. They are working individually on number problems designed to consolidate concepts about place value which were introduced earlier in the week. The problems are presented on several coloured cards and they must reproduce and answer them in their workbooks. Izzah is tackling problem five which is different to the ones he's successfully completed so far. He realizes that all the problems on this card are new to him. He becomes anxious and says to himself, 'I can't do these ones'. He looks around to see how others, especially Nathan, are coping. He realizes that Nathan is on the next set of problems. He goes on to the next card which contains problems like all the others he has done so far, but he is upset and anxious so he gets several wrong. Nathan decided to skip the problems on the blue card and to do the familiar ones on the red and yellow cards first. He comes back to the blue card and has a go. He tries out different strategies but they don't seem to work for him. He realizes that the three number problems are similar in format. He approaches the teacher and explains to her that he's stuck and that he can't work out how to do this type of problem. She quickly realizes that the blue cards contain symbols and problems that the children haven't yet encountered and that these cards got mixed up with the other cards by mistake. She withdraws them and explains to the group that they will be able to do these problems in a few months' time when they have learned some new number skills. The different reactions of Izzah and Nathan to this situation are typical.

These examples demonstrate that people vary in how they deal with what life has to offer, and more specifically in their dispositions to learning. It would seem that these differences start early, in some cases before formal school experience (Smiley and Dweck 1994; Claxton 1999) and, although they are not set in stone, they can endure throughout life. Dispositions are learned responses that are dependent upon the opportunities and constraints available in each new setting. And these opportunities and constraints are jointly produced by the individual, peers and teachers, and are influenced by the sets of relationships among the relevant individuals in the particular setting, and of course by the activity in hand.

The definition of learning disposition offered by Carr and Claxton (2002: 12) is helpful: 'A disposition is neither unique to a specific situation nor generally manifested across all situations. It is a tendency to respond or learn in a certain way that is somewhat, but incompletely, 'disembedded' from particular constellations of personal, social and material detail'. The 'not entirely disembedded' part is important, we think, for this leaves open the impact of context, the expectations of the participants – learners, teachers, parents etc. – and the assumptions about 'the way things are done around here'.

What are important learning dispositions? Several writers have come up with lists. For example, Goleman (1995) talks about confidence, curiosity, intentionality, self-control, relatedness, communication and cooperation. Claxton (1999) refers to resilience, resourcefulness and reflectiveness. Carr and Claxton (2002) refer to resilience, playfulness and reciprocity. Harvard's Project Zero (Krechersky 1991) describes persistence, attention to detail, confidence and many more. Several elements in the QCA's FSP correspond with some of these dispositions (see e.g. Table 11.1 above). To illustrate further, we will consider Claxton's three – resilience, resourcefulness and reflectiveness – with reference to our two scenarios above. First we should point out that there remain unresolved issues about what might constitute appropriate learning dispositions (Katz 2002) and about how best to assess them (Allal 2002).

On the basis of the very limited evidence of the children above, what can we say about their learning dispositions? First we should reiterate the need to observe children in a variety of different contexts before drawing conclusions about them as learners. We have only given our readers an account of one observation of the children and this would be most inadequate as a basis for judging their dispositions. We simply use our two scenarios here to elaborate for our readers what we mean by dispositions rather than to claim to offer an insightful account of the children as learners.

### Resilience

Drawing on Claxton (1999) Katie and Nathan demonstrate more resilience and robustness as learners than Fiona and Izzah. They are able to handle strangeness, they are more adventurous, they are better able to cope with uncertainty and they are more willing to have a go. From the positive expression of her mother, Katie not only obtained permission, but the courage, to explore, and she knows when to pull back. Fiona, on the other hand, is not willing to tolerate the feelings that go along with learning and so she is less inclined to lay the foundations for the development of resilience. She and Izzah are more fragile or brittle in how they respond to the world. Izzah has a lower tolerance of frustration and quickly gets upset when the unpredictable happens. The degree of resilience that learners display is bound up with their beliefs about themselves, their efficacy, beliefs about ability, beliefs about the nature of learning and knowledge and most importantly, as we noted above, about the context in which the activity is happening, which includes the expectations of others.

### Resourcefulness

Resourcefulness involves searching for new ways to tackle a problem or cope with a new situation. Resourceful learners have many tools in their learning toolkit, says Claxton (1999). Nathan stuck with the task he faced and discovered all three problems were similar in format but that despite his efforts their resolution eluded him. He then sought help. Izzah, on the other hand, quickly gave up, got upset and even failed to solve familiar problems successfully. He could not tolerate the confusion and frustration presented by the new situation. Resourcefulness is about knowing what to do when you don't know what to do. It is about being able to make good use of external resources, like the people around you, and internal resources like language and imagination.

### Reflectiveness

To be resilient and resourceful, apparently, is not enough. One also needs to be strategic and to know oneself. This means knowing one's strengths and weaknesses, having the ability to check out the situation and decide how best to proceed. Nathan quickly decided to complete all the familiar tasks that were set for him first, then to revisit the more demanding and unfamiliar problems. Having pondered these problems and tried out a number of approaches, he sensibly sought assistance. He possessed the necessary emotional tolerance (Goleman 1995) to stick with the task long enough to succeed had he had the necessary background knowledge to accomplish the task.

These three features of learning constantly and positively reinforce each other to produce what Claxton calls '*learning power*'. This means that the more resilient, resourceful and reflective learners are, they more they build their own capacity for learning and the more confident learners they become. Obviously, if one tries longer and harder, the more likely it is that one will solve the problem or discover a new way to resolve the issue. As one learns one is becoming a more powerful learner – one's 'learning to learn is on an upward spiral' (Claxton 1999: 3). Fiona and Izzah are less adventurous, less curious, less skilful and less aware than Katie or Nathan – they have fewer opportunities to learn and their 'learnability' of learning itself is curtailed accordingly. Fiona perceives the world as more threatening than it actually is and so misses opportunities to have fun and learn new things. Similarly, Izzah gets upset easily and gives up, thus forfeiting the chance to develop his learning power.

Those learners, therefore, who are more fearful of ambiguity and uncertainty withdraw more quickly, thus missing out on opportunities that would foster learnability, and together these two behaviour patterns become self-fulfilling prophecies. Learners themselves 'slow down' or 'speed up' their own progress (Claxton 1999: 260).

## Beliefs, expectations, feelings and context

Learning power does not develop automatically and people's dispositions to learning are grounded in their beliefs about a whole host of aspects of learning – beliefs that have been learned from their particular experiences of life.

A most fascinating aspect of learning is that a) learning itself is learnable and b) the early years are tremendously significant in terms of shaping the kind of future learner one becomes. Underlying and explaining the person's orientation to learning is a myriad of beliefs – often unconsciously held – about learning, knowledge, ability and intelligence. These tacitly held beliefs are based in turn on the messages received from the setting or learning context, from the home, the media, schooling, peers and the entire environment of the young person as well as, crucially, how those messages are interpreted and understood. For example, in school life, different understandings of learning are realized through different patterns of classroom communication (Hall 1995, 2002; Mercer 1995; Hall *et al.* 1999). The important point is that the way children feel about themselves as learners is learned.

On the basis of a considerable number of experimental studies, several researchers have identified two major orientations to learning (Wigfield *et al.* 1998). One orientation is characterized as holding ego-orientated goals; the other, as holding task-orientated goals. Individuals with ego-orientated goals seek to maximize positive evaluations of their competence from teachers, parents, carers, peers etc. and minimize negative ones. Their overarching concern is looking smart and perhaps outperforming others. Questions such as 'Will I look clever?' and 'Can I beat my peers?' reflect ego-orientated goals. In contrast, learners with task-orientated goals focus on mastering the task and increasing their skill. Questions such as 'How can I do this task?' and 'What will I learn?' reflect task-orientated goals. A third type of goal orientation is work avoidance. As its label suggests, this refers to avoiding work and those who are so orientated often fear failure, have low levels of confidence in themselves as learners and lack determination and 'stickability'.

For the task-orientated learner, hard work and having a go are important. Since they are not ego-orientated, they go directly for generating strategies that may solve the problem or complete the task. They tend to be good attenders to the task, they get intellectually absorbed and emotionally rapt. Unsurprisingly, there is consistent support in the research literature (Wigfield *et al.* 1988) for the benefits of pursuing task-orientated or learning-orientated goals. In addition, it would appear that when children believe they are competent, they are more likely to be motivated for intrinsic reasons. And their beliefs are hugely influenced by the messages (overt and covert) delivered by those around them. Positive competence beliefs, intrinsic motivation and learning goals lead to greater determination and stickability, and to the selection of more challenging tasks and higher levels of engagement in different activities (Wigfield *et al.* 1988).

Interestingly then, those who need it most have the least practice since they, like Fiona and Izzah, resist and miss out on vital opportunities to enhance their learning power. They tend to revert prematurely to a defensive mode. So, it would seem, to those who have shall yet more be given. It is easy to understand how some children get into a spiral of failure.

## Promoting and recognizing positive learning dispositions

Recent research on teacher effectiveness shows that 'coaching' is key (e.g. Taylor *et al.* 2000). Coaching refers to the use of structuring comments, the probing of pupil responses and scaffolded instruction. The more effective teachers in several studies of effective literacy teaching, for example (Hall and Harding 2003) exhibit a preference for coaching over telling. Claxton (1999) also refers to coaching and to the role of the 'learning coach' in promoting positive learning dispositions. The central role of the 'learning coach', he says, is to help the learner to explore and exploit the resources of the environment and of the mind, to help the learner to be perceptive and reflective about the possibilities for support and to be effective at making use of such support. The learning coach, he says, whether in the home or school environment, creates a climate that says to the young child, 'There is something to be learned and you can make things happen': there is freedom to make decisions and take control within a structured, secure and supportive environment.

One way of being a good learning coach is to keep ownership with the learner. Learners need scaffolding, but not too much. Getting the balance right is key. Tasks that reflect 'easy difficulty' seem to be best. Allowing children to grapple with difficulty for a while, even to take on a bit of distress, teaches them that learning involves struggle and that frequently the intrinsic rewards, such as the sense of achievement, are in proportion to that struggle. The learning coach needs to ensure that ownership of the task or the learning remains with the learner. In practice, this means 'nudging' in the form of tentative commentary about how to proceed when the learner needs rescuing (i.e. when they are is stuck or flagging). This approach fosters resilience.

Learning is maximized when the enabling adult participates in the activity and when interactions follow from the child's self-initiated actions (Claxton 1999). Drawing attention to the effects of the child's action by saying things like 'Now I think you've got the hang of it' and reminding the learner of other approaches that might work are more advantageous than providing lots of information or too much praise.

The job of the learning coach is to help learners select and use the best tools for the task in hand. The aim is to equip them with an orientation to seek out the relevant resources in their environment, and to help them to be perceptive about the possibilities for support around them as well as to be perceptive about what it is they already know and can do (reflectiveness).

The learning coach also needs to encourage appropriate help-seeking. This involves helping learners in a) deciding when to seek help – when they have tried to solve the problem on their own; b) figuring out what and whom to ask; and c) developing good questions to obtain the needed help. Despite the learner-centred model that curriculum designers aspire to, research findings suggest that many children view help-seeking as an admission that they cannot complete a problem on their own (Wigfield *et al.* 1998). Being a resourceful learner involves using your internal and external resources (including the parent, teacher or peers) to problem solve. Unsurprisingly, children are more likely to seek help when their teachers are warm and supportive and when they organize learning or teaching around learning or task goals rather than performance or ego goals, and when they work in small collaborative groups rather than in large, whole-class groups (Wigfield *et al.* 1998).

A good learning coach can reflect back to learners some sense of their take on the learning task and context. They may confirm that the task is difficult; they may verbalize feelings (e.g. 'I can see you're excited about doing this'); they may provide encouragement when the learner feels challenged 'Come on, you know that word'). Sue, the teacher we mentioned in Chapter 5, exemplifies this approach. She develops reflectiveness and a respect for the feelings of learning and the feelings of the learner.

Praise can be dangerous. Too much praise (and especially extrinsic rewards such as stars and certificates) take away some of the intrinsic motivation for learning; they tend to reduce persistence and undermine resilience; and they remove independence and undermine self-esteem (see Dweck 1999). One study showed how the allocation of a *'Good Player Certificate'* to nursery children resulted in the children's play being less active and creative, while another study which examined the impact of teacher praise on children's drawing and painting found that the children started to produce work that was increasingly unoriginal.

We will summarize this guidance by quoting from Claxton (1999: 270), who draws on the work of Margaret Carr, one of the architects of New Zealand's innovative curriculum, Te Whariki. He says:

> The learning coach's eye stays firmly on the expansion of children's learning power. It doesn't matter so much whether this morning's fascination is with jigsaw puzzles whilst the afternoon's is with next door's new kitten, and tomorrow's is with naming the characters in a story-book. It doesn't even matter if they are not interested in books

or sums yet; there is plenty of learning-to-learn that can be done in the meantime. The top priority is to guide activity, model approaches and offer suggestions so that children keep expanding their stock of things to do when they don't know what to do, and their ability to stay intelligently engaged with difficult and novel predicaments.

## Conclusion

The emphasis of the new assessment policy in the early years on learning dispositions is to be welcomed. In this chapter we have taken just that one aspect and discussed it in some detail. We now turn more explicitly to ways of describing and assessing children's learning dispositions.

# 12 Playful Learning, Learning Stories and Making Assessment Visible in the Early Years

## Introduction

The following extract is from notes made by the second author in an infant school. It offers evidence of ability to empathize and have concern for others' needs in a reception class (5-year-olds) – a key element of the FSP.

> I was visiting an infants' school and passed by a group of four reception children playing in a Wendy house. They were running a travel agency and had been positioned by their teacher near the entrance to their classroom, in the corridor, so that they could benefit from opportunities to talk, in a secure environment, with staff and children who were passing by. I stopped and enquired about suitable holidays for myself and my family and supplied a few details about the kind of activities we liked. They showed me various brochures and I asked which holiday they would recommend. I received a lot of help, particularly regarding children's likes and dislikes on holiday. I thanked them and placed my order and said that when I returned from seeing the Year 1 children in the next classroom I would collect my tickets if that was all right with them. I then

moved on down the corridor, but before I had reached the classroom door a worried little boy ran after me. I turned at his request to see a concerned expression and to hear him say, 'It's only play you know.' Taken aback I eventually replied, 'Yes, I realized it was but thanks for explaining.' He returned to the Wendy house. I continued into the Year 1 classroom but his remark stayed with me. I had been too effective in my role-play and he was confused as to whether I understood the rules which operated in his classroom. I remain impressed that he felt that it was important that I should understand the situation.

What an interesting and spontaneous demonstration of this boy's ability to take the perspective of another. Not only were these children engaging with the needs of others through the kind of holidays adults and children might enjoy, but also with the more immediate need (as one boy perceived it) of the visitor to understand what was really going on. This chapter is being written at a time (May 2003) when the Secretary of State for Education and Skills, Charles Clarke, proclaims that 'enjoyment is the birthright of every child', that 'children learn better when they are excited and engaged ... when there is joy in what they are doing, they learn to love learning' (DfES 2003). Infant teachers have known and acted upon such principles for years, although governments' preoccupation with standards and attainment in a limited number of areas in the past decade or so has curtailed their adherence to these principles. As we said in the previous chapter, the emphasis on engagement, involvement, playfulness and learning orientations evident in the FSP and in the ELGs is a welcome shift.

In this chapter we take forward some of the issues about learning dispositions introduced in the previous chapter. We use examples and critical incidents or 'learning stories' to illustrate how learning dispositions might be assessed in a formative way. We draw on several recent and important research initiatives including a research and development project by Margaret Carr and her colleagues in New Zealand, Project Spectrum within Harvard's Project Zero and some approaches used in preschools in Reggio Emilia, Italy. We draw mostly on the work of Margaret Carr and her team who, over the past several years have been developing an assessment framework to suit New Zealand's innovative early childhood curriculum (see Carr and May 1993; Carr 1999, 2001; Podmore and Carr 1999; and May and Carr 2000). They argued that the New Zealand curriculum, which is based on sociocultural and ecological principles of learning, called for a different approach to assessment. The curriculum that their assessment approach sought to fit is based on four key principles: the empowerment of the learner; the recognition of the holistic way children learn; links with community and family; and recognition of the way children learn through reciprocal relationships with people, places and things. Based on evaluations, action research and case studies in several early childhood settings, Margaret Carr and her team developed what they termed 'the learning story framework'. We draw on this work below.

## Useful assessments of learning dispositions

What kind of an account of learning do we need? Carr (2001: 22) has argued that 'learning dispositions are about responsive and reciprocal relationships between the individual and the environment'. She says they form a repertoire of 'familiar and privileged processes of contribution and communication'. She goes on to say that 'learning dispositions will be about becoming a participant in a learning place and taking a critical approach to that participation' (p. 22). All of this is captured in the above scenario. The playful child is intensely involved in the activity, but is also capable of taking a critical approach to his and others' participation. This learning disposition of (deep) involvement is situated in and interconnected with action and activity. The notion of 'learner in action' with others, as opposed to individual alone, is not easily represented in tick sheets of performance indicators because such assessments are 'empty of context'.

However, qualitative, narrative accounts can attempt to do justice to the complexity of development and learning. Narrative accounts can reflect the perspective of the learner in that assessment can be made in the knowledge of what the learner set out to do, rather than in terms of some predetermined outcome. Narrative accounts can capture moments of development that acknowledge its unpredictability. By taking many observations over time, narrative accounts have the capacity to offer insights into a child's continuity and progression in relation to dispositions – for example, the inclination to risk error, to persist in the face of difficulty, to find pleasure in exploration, to remain focused, to concentrate, to become deeply involved, to communicate and to take responsibility. Narrative accounts allow for collaborative interpretations including interpretations by learners themselves which play a key role in contributing to the development of positive dispositions.

Assessment then is part and parcel of the child's involvement over time. To foster the demonstration of these positive dispositions a rich learning and play environment is needed, containing engaging materials, games, puzzles and learning areas. In Project Spectrum (Krechersky 1991: 43), for example, practitioners are encouraged to notice how children play and work, whether, for example, the child is:

- easily engaged or reluctant to engage in an activity;
- confident or tentative;
- playful or serious;
- focused or distracted;

- persistent or frustrated by the task or the game;
- reflective about own work or impulsive;
- apt to work slowly or apt to work quickly.

They notice how a child:

- responds to visual/auditory/kinesthetic cues;
- demonstrates a planful approach;
- brings a personal agenda or strength to the activity;
- finds humour in an activity;
- uses materials in unexpected ways;
- shows pride in accomplishments;
- is curious about materials;
- shows concern over 'correct' answers;
- focuses on interaction with adults;
- transforms the task/material.

Rather than a tick sheet that invites a 'yes' or 'no' response to such issues, stories of a child's learning can 'capture the complexity of situated learning strategies plus motivation' (Carr 2001: 95). They can integrate various dimensions of learning – the social, the emotional and the cognitive. Margaret Carr talks about the 'learning story approach' which consists of observations in everyday settings designed to produce a cumulative record of qualitative snapshots of learning dispositions. These are episodes of achievement that over time build an authentic picture of the learner that can be shared, not only with other practitioners and parents, but – crucially – with the learners themselves. She refined this approach with practitioners in early childhood settings in New Zealand who were encouraged to collect 'critical incidents' of children doing the following: taking an interest, being involved, persisting with difficulty or uncertainty, expressing an idea or a feeling. A series of stories over time for individual children were examined for patterns and progress. Learning stories were kept in portfolios along with photographs, children's comments and samples of their work. The next section provides some examples of this in action.

## Learning stories in action

Carr tells how in one childcare centre of 4-year-olds the practitioners were using a checklist to record which skills had been attained and which had not. Particular skills were ticked or crossed, and dated, and the adults discussed the crossed items. On the basis of the deficits identified, activities were planned and interventions made. She tells how one child, Bruce, who was frequently aggressive and unhappy and who engendered fear in other children, had crosses against all the social items on the checklist. The practitioners used a behaviourist approach with Bruce in that they noted the context in which his aggressive behaviour took place and recorded the antecedents and the consequences of his actions. Bruce got more than his fair share of adult attention.

However, within the research study, practitioners were encouraged to document those occasions when Bruce was taking an interest, being involved, persisting with difficulty or uncertainty, expressing an idea or a feeling and taking responsibility. Carr explains how the practitioners still had to cope with Bruce's aggressive outbursts but that they began to encourage Bruce's willingness and ability to communicate with others in more acceptable ways and to assume some responsibility in negotiations and relationships. The following learning stories about Bruce are typical of the approach Carr developed with the teachers (2001: 98–101).

### Learning story 1

Louise and Bruce have laid out mattresses on the hill in the sun, and have had discussions about which one they will each lie on.

*Bruce [to Louise]*: I'll be the dad.

*Louise*: No, Jeanie's the dad.

Bruce approaches Jeanie, with his face close to hers.

*Jeanie*: I'm the daddy.

*Bruce*: There can be two daddies.

*Jeanie*: No.

*Bruce*: I'll be the mate, eh?

This appears to be acceptable to Jeanie and Louise (they don't say 'No') and they play together amicably for some time.

This is a story that is taken to provide evidence of Bruce's learning to negotiate. Such negotiation seems to be confined initially to sociodramatic play that includes Louise, like the above. But the staff expect that such behaviour can be extended in a short time to include other children, and this they believe is a marked improvement on Bruce's earlier and more typical behaviour which consisted of hitting and pushing other children.

### Learning story 2

Bruce believes (perhaps accurately) that Amy has scratched him: he tells her he doesn't like it, chases her, and explains to Milly (a teacher) that he didn't hit her (Amy). Both Milly and another teacher give positive feedback.

This apparently was one of the first times that Bruce seemed to take control of his actions and the teacher affirmed his behaviour by her reaction.

### Learning story 3
Bruce asks Annie to look after his block and animal construction, and she attempts to do so. At one stage he says: 'Annie, it's okay, it looked after itself!'

This incident in interpreted by the staff to indicate Bruce's acceptable mode of communication.

### Learning story 4
This morning Bruce announces: 'I'm a good pirate and I save people.'

While Bruce can occasionally cause disturbances, the staff notice his increasing willingness to frame his play and his stories, and more particularly his identity within them, in more positive and empathetic ways than he had done previously. They discuss Bruce's actions and they plan ways of encouraging him to take responsibility by playing with Louise (with whom he plays agreeably) and with others. They decide to encourage him to 'reframe his pirate stories (saving people and finding treasure, rather than killing and taking hostages at the point of a sword)' (Carr 2001: 99). The staff note how Bruce claims areas of the room, like the sandpit, as 'his' and tries to prevent others from using them, even when he himself is elsewhere.

### Learning story 5
Bruce in the block corner.
He builds an enclosure around wild animals.
Very involved.

A member of staff records several episodes of Bruce's play and one in particular, where he 'built an enclosure' around several children and an adult. He pretended to be a tiger but later he was the protector of tigers.

### Learning story 6
In the family corner, Bruce starts off being a tiger. I (teacher) suggest that I am a tiger as well, and I encourage him to make a larger enclosure around us all (I noticed that he had made an enclosure around wild animals this morning). Other children are playing a domestic kitchen, 'making breakfast' game, and take no notice of Bruce. He makes an enclosure around us all.

What is especially interesting about the way the staff notice, record and discuss these episodes is how these same stories can be fed back to children to provide powerful vehicles for recalling events, for talking about feelings and for articulating important learning dispositions, like taking responsibility, responding in acceptable ways, being involved and so on.

The project sets out a four-part assessment process (Podmore and Carr 1999). First, 'describing' occurs when the practitioners identify the learning to be assessed. They are especially interested in assessing and promoting robust learning dispositions. Second, 'documenting' occurs in a range of ways and, importantly, for a range of audiences – the child, the practitioners, the family and outside agencies. Examples of positive behaviour are considered important ways of communicating to the child and to the family what is valued in the childhood setting. Third, 'discussing' occurs with the child, with another practitioner or the family and this is considered a crucial part of the assessment process. Fourth, 'deciding' is about next steps in terms of the child's development.

## Learning stories as a pedagogical tool

As Carr's research and development project progressed and as the participants in it continued to document learning in the way briefly described above, the documented learning came to be used as scripts or stories that became part of the curriculum. The stories became longer and themes in children's work and play could be highlighted, shared and enjoyed. Carr (2001: 141) says 'the stories have become cultural artefacts and literacy events' and children request them to be read again and again. As one might imagine, the children not only thoroughly enjoyed stories in which they themselves were the central characters, but they also benefited from personally meaningful contexts to discuss the deep involvement, effort, persistence, responsibility and collaboration that they were encouraged to demonstrate.

Carr's research provides evidence of how learning stories are a pedagogical tool for the transformation of participation, by which she means they have the potential to encourage deeper learning. Learning stories are credit rather than deficit focused. As such they provide a vehicle for demonstrating what learning really matters and for transmitting the classroom culture to all participants. They are also able to 'reframe incoming narratives' and here Carr refers to a 'narrative therapy' approach to counselling where the counsellor is not seen as a fixer or an expert who can solve the problem. Rather the counsellor and the client together '"story" the client's experience' (Carr 2001: 103), they search for 'glimmers of an alternative narrative'. In this way 'problems are interpreted as social constructions that can be changed'. The point Carr makes is that such stories, whether in the therapy or classroom setting, have not had an audience before and the influence of a significant audience is a key aspect in the construction and reconstruction of life stories.

It would seem that the sharing and the building of collective knowledge are vital ingredients of assessing *for* (as opposed to *of*) learning. This is also borne out by other research on assessment in early years settings. In a collaboration between Project Spectrum at the Harvard Graduate School of Education and the Municipal Infant-toddler Centers and Preschools of Reggio Emilia (Turner and Krechevsky 2003) the kinds of principles underlying Carr's work are also in evidence (e.g. the importance of the learner's perspective, the collaborative interpretation of evidence and the emphasis on learning dispositions). The collaborative project is called 'Making Learning Visible' (Project Zero and Reggio Children 2001).

Like the participants in the New Zealand study, the Reggio Emilia approach is one that places considerable emphasis on documenting learning and sharing learning, especially group learning, with learners and adults through photos and displays of work incorporating adult summaries, somewhat akin to Carr's learning stories. This moves learning from the private to the public realm and allows children and adults to reflect on, evaluate and build on their previous efforts (Turner and Krechevsky 2003). Words and pictures are used to capture the emotions of learning and to acknowledge the social dimension of learning. Most importantly, such displays make images of group learning visible in the classroom, thus fostering a sense of group identity. Such images serve as a memory for what happened. Children routinely discuss their work with partners.

Interestingly, this project noted how US educators, in comparison to their Italian counterparts in Reggio Emilia, tend to place more emphasis on the promotion of autonomy and individuation in their learning. The Reggio Emilia approach challenges these values, claiming that it is precisely the group setting that allows individuals to develop distinctive identities. This is how one Italian child explained the value of group learning: '[in a group] your brain works better. Because your ideas when you say them out loud keep coming together, and when all the ideas come together, you get a gigantic idea! You can think better in a group' (Project Zero and Reggio Children 2001: 323). This quote reveals something of this child's identity as a learner. It also reminds us that what we ask children to do, how we ask them to do it and how we assess it, are inseparable from the kind of learners we are asking them to become.

## Conclusion

A storied approach to assessment is more likely than other ways we have encountered to offer respectful accounts of learners and their learning as well as accounts that support their future learning. It offers a way of 'seeing' learners as opposed to just 'looking' at them to in order to fit them into categories. This type of approach has been used by several researchers in the

UK (e.g. Barrs *et al.* 1992; Blenkin and Kelly 1992; Torrance and Pryor 1998; Pollard and Filer 1999; Filer and Pollard 2000) and in the USA (e.g. Dyson 1997; Hicks 2001). It is an approach to describing and assessing learning that we believe merits much more dissemination and application.

# 13 Level Descriptions and Opportunities for Formative Assessment

## with Austin Harding

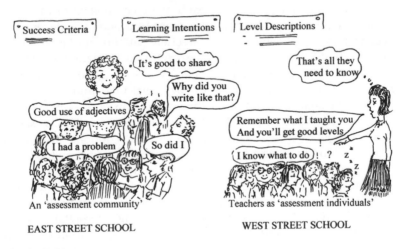

EAST STREET SCHOOL                WEST STREET SCHOOL

## Introduction

This chapter[1] considers the possible links between summative and formative assessment. Any assessment is only as good as the use to which it is put, and assessment information, including that obtained via SATs and teacher assessment, can be used in a way that informs teaching and learning – i.e. can be used formatively. In this chapter we consider the way teacher assessment is being used in some schools to feed back into the pedagogy of the classroom. We have already described official policy on assessment (Chapter 2) and we have emphasized the importance of helping learners understand how their

[1] This chapter draws on a reseach paper by Kathy Hall and Austin Harding entitled 'Level descriptions and teacher assessment: towards a community of assessment practice' which was published in 2002 in *Educational Research*, 40(1):1–6. This project was funded by the ESRC (R000222373).

work is judged (Chapter 5). A major focus of this chapter is how teachers themselves share interpretations of standards and success criteria with reference to level descriptions and teacher assessment. The focus of this chapter is on the mechanisms and structures some schools use to promote and share assessment criteria with staff, pupils and parents.

## Level descriptions as assessment criteria

Level descriptions are summary, prose statements that describe the types and range of performance which pupils working towards a particular level of the National Curriculum should demonstrate. There is a scale of eight levels, designed to facilitate progression, for each major component of the curriculum. Teachers are asked to consider the range of a pupil's achievements in each curriculum component or, more precisely, 'attainment target'. Judging which level 'best fits' a child's performance for each attainment target involves cross-checking against adjacent levels in the scale and considering the balance of strengths and weaknesses for each particular child.

As we have argued several times throughout this book, any assessment criteria will need to be interpreted by those who use them. This is especially the case for those as loosely framed as the level descriptions. Just as pupils need to obtain an understanding of how their work is judged, so too teachers need to share an understanding of the level descriptions. It would be a mistake to imagine that the words laid down in the written level descriptions are interpreted in the same way by all teachers who use them (Wiliam 1998). Rather, it is through an on-going process of sharing interpretation of level descriptions in actual contexts of application that their meaning is made clear. We share the view that quality in communities of assessment practice can only be defined as the consensus of those teachers involved in making assessment judgements. For assessments to be useful, credible and meaningful, there needs to be a collective agreement borne out of professional dialogue and the sharing of perspectives and working practices. We also share the view that obtaining absolute objectivity in educational assessment is impossible. However, as we already noted, this does not mean that we shouldn't try to maximize the trustworthiness of the judgements we make of our pupils' learning.

## A study of practice

One of the lessons we (should) have learned since the advent of National Curriculum assessment is that assessment results have meaning for individuals through the interpretation of others. It the use to which assessment information is put that is crucial for learners – this is often termed 'consequential validity'. What use do teachers make of teacher assessment and level descriptions? How, if at all, does the process of allocating levels to pupils' achievements in teacher assessment inform teaching and pupils' learning? In a research project spanning two years and funded by the Economic and Social Research Council (ESRC), we sought to answer these questions. We refer to aspects of that project in this chapter (see Hall and Harding 1999 and 2002 for more details).

Key Stage 1 teachers in six schools from six different LEAs in the north of England participated in a study about the use of level descriptions. The schools represented a variety of settings and types of catchment. We interviewed all the Year 2 teachers and the assessment coordinators in all six schools in two consecutive years, amounting to 48 interviews in total. In the second year of the project we also interviewed one Year 3 teacher in each school. We interviewed LEA assessment advisers (associated with the schools) in each year of the project. We also collected, or were shown, documentary evidence such as portfolios, record sheets and school and LEA policy documents, and we observed teachers as they discussed the allocation of levels based on their teacher assessments.

## A framework for describing teachers' practice

We identified two contrasting tendencies in our evidence on the process of interpreting and applying level descriptions for teacher assessment. These tendencies reflect two distinct approaches to teacher assessment, at school level, and we term them *collaborative* and *individualistic*. On the basis of our evidence we could distinguish between those schools that exhibited many of the features associated with *an assessment community* and those where the style was of individual teachers tending to work largely in isolation from one another. In this section of the chapter we offer an overview of that framework, while remaining sections of the chapter will offer a more detailed account of what teachers do.

Table 13.1 summarizes the major tendencies that distinguish one approach from another. Two of our schools – East Street and West Street respectively – show these contrasting tendencies. The remaining four schools (Easterly, Central, Middling and Westerly) could be positioned closer to one or other extreme in relation to some or all of the key elements of assessment that we identified as significant – namely, goals, tools and processes, personnel and value system. For the purposes of this chapter, we concentrate mainly on the two most contrasting schools.

East Street School conforms most closely to an 'assessment community'. It is a large inner-city primary school of 400-plus pupils, all but 5 per cent of

**Table 13.1** 'Assessment communities' and 'assessment individuals'

| | Collaborative (East Street School) | Individualistic (West Street School) |
|---|---|---|
| Goals | Compliant and accepting | Reluctant compliance and resistance |
| Tools and processes | 1 Level descriptions: interpretation is shared<br>2 Portfolio: in active use<br>3 Exemplification materials: owned by teachers; a mixture of school-devised and QCA materials<br>4 Evidence: planned collection; variety of modes; assessment embedded in teaching and learning; emphasis on the process<br>5 Common language of assessment<br>6 Commitment to moderation | 1 Level descriptions: little or no sharing of interpretations<br>2 Portfolio: dormant<br>3 Exemplification materials: QCA not used; commercially produced materials used by some individuals<br>4 Evidence: not used much; assessment often bolted onto learning and teaching; emphasis on products<br>5 Uncertainty/confusion about terms<br>6 Weak or non-existent moderation |
| Personnel | Whole school; aspirations to enlarge the assessment community to include pupils, parents and other teachers | Year 2 teachers as individuals; no real grasp of the potential for enlarging the assessment community |
| Value system | Assessment seen as useful, necessary and integral to teaching and learning; made meaningful through collaboration | Assessment seen as 'imposed' and not meaningful at the level of the class teacher |

whom are from ethnic minority backgrounds. The recently built school is located in an economically disadvantaged area of a northern city. Its staff shares the purposes and goals of National Curriculum assessment (NCA) in general and of teacher assessment in particular. It shares a set of processes like moderation and level descriptions interpretation for achieving these goals. It seeks a common usage of a range of tools, such as school portfolios, to help staff in their assessment tasks. It strives to include pupils, parents and other teachers as part of that assessment community and it shares a set of values about the importance and manageability of these tasks.

West Street School, in contrast, reluctantly complies with the goals of NCA. This is a larger than average primary school serving a varied socio-economic area in a northern city. Pupils are drawn from a mixture of privately owned and council maintained housing and the school has a sizeable number of pupils from educationally disadvantaged backgrounds. Teachers work largely in isolation from each other in interpreting and implementing assessment goals and, especially, in interpreting level descriptions and using exemplification material and evidence. There is no real attempt to involve interested groups, like parents and pupils, in assessment discussions. The school tends to view NCA as an unhelpful, arduous intrusion.

## Portfolios, evidence and exemplification material

All the LEA advisers we interviewed emphasized the use of a school portfolio to demonstrate the evidence needed for the attainment of the different levels in the various curriculum areas. The QCA exemplification material, they suggested, should inform and support the process of portfolio production. One adviser also suggested that work samples should be not only levelled but annotated in such a way that the level was justified and the 'next steps' for the achievement of the subsequent level specified. In this way both summative and formative purposes could be served. The advisers also discussed the use of individual pupil portfolios for the collection of annotated evidence of children's work. All six advisers spoke at considerable length about the importance of drawing conclusions on the basis of evidence from different sources (e.g. observation, questioning, individual written work, group tasks and so on), and about how teachers might collect and keep some examples or accounts of pupils' work to evidence their judgements. Furthermore, they showed us materials and guidance they typically share with teachers on their assessment courses.

However, our interviews with the teachers testified to the limited access they had to the great deal of expertise that has undoubtedly been built up at LEA level about assessment in general and teacher assessment in particular. In such circumstances, teachers are left to depend on one another for support in the interpretation of assessment criteria for teacher assessment.

In four of our six schools, teacher assessment was presented as the business of the whole staff and individual efforts were, to varying degrees, supported by a collective machinery that involved discussion and decisions on the processes described in Table 13.1. In these same schools the school assessment coordinators talked about collective action as well as individual responsibility to share and agree practices. The assessment coordinators in these schools emphasized that NCA, including teacher assessment, is a wholeschool issue and not just the responsibility of teachers of Years 2 and 6.

However, with the exception of East Street, all such collaboration occurred at the end of the teaching day and increasingly competed for time with a host of other initiatives. In the two remaining schools the assessment coordinators acknowledged that teacher assessment had taken a *back seat* and that as a result procedures to enhance the credibility of teacher judgements were no longer firmly in place.

In interview, the Year 2 teachers corroborated what their school assessment coordinators said, explaining that they simply did not have time. However, these teachers were critical of what they saw as a general lack of support for teacher assessment from their colleagues. In both these schools, teacher assessment was, in practice, the task of individual teachers with little or no collaboration with colleagues. For example, when discussing ways of familiarizing the whole school staff with assessment issues and ways in which this might be done, a teacher in West Street referred to the school portfolio that was developed many years before as part of agreement trialing but its datedness, she lamented, now means it is no longer a meaningful document for staff. A picture emerges in West Street of a dead, underused portfolio with little or no potential to focus a range of teacher-teacher, teacher-parent and teacher-child interactions. The teachers perceived themselves as working alone. In so far as they shared interpretations of evidence and criteria, they did so rarely and on an *ad hoc* basis, and only the Year 2 teachers were involved.

East Street Primary School is exceptional in that it is not a case of teachers always snatching time after the school day. As one teacher put it: 'we had time given to do it'. Here she was referring to the headteacher's decision to employ supply staff to release a small group of teachers to discuss how they would interpret the level descriptions and the evidence needed to support the allocation of levels. In this school, horizontal year group collaboration is in place as is a vertical whole-school acceptance of its assessment responsibilities and the need for a common collaborative approach. Our observation of a moderation meeting of teachers in this school demonstrated their awareness of how a pupil's work or performance on a set task or even series of tasks cannot be considered in isolation from the context in which those tasks occur. This would include the network of relationships in operation in the classroom and the support on offer.

Filer and Pollard (2000) talk, in their work, about the complexities of 'knowing' a child. How a teacher 'knows a child', they suggest, is bound up with and dependent upon features of the classroom contexts that the teacher creates. These classroom contexts in turn can have enormous effects on a pupil's engagement with learning and relationships and consequently can have dramatic effects on the assessments that derive from that engagement and set of relationships (see also Chapter 4). What came across from our interaction with the staff in East Street was their apparent assumption that knowledge of individual pupils cannot be 'read off' in a straightforward way. The teachers here were prepared to discuss and share interpretation and justify the levels they had allocated. There was an assumption that assessment is far from an exact science. As Filer and Pollard eloquently argue, assessments of pupils' behaviour, achievements, attitudes to work etc. are at best 're-presentations' of the individual. The teachers in East Street were coming round to that way of thinking about assessment.

In East Street, there was an emergent recognition that the pupil portfolio might have a wider usage than simply as a repository of achievements for the Year 3 teacher. It was beginning to be seen as having the potential for linking an individual teacher with other teachers, with pupils and with their parents. The collection and collation of annotated, levelled work into pupil portfolios was seen as being a very useful focus around which more numerous and meaningful teacher-teacher, teacher-parent and teacher-child discussions might be sustained. The impression one got here was that assessment is a contested business always open to interpretation: it is something to be talked about, shared, interpreted and reinterpreted.

It is noteworthy that all six schools in the study remain isolated from other schools in their regions. We found that inter-school collaboration about teacher assessment and level descriptions was non-existent in both years of the research project – this had been a feature in all six schools in the early days of NCA. Interviewees regretted the lack of funding that led to the demise of this, all having experienced it as an important means of professional development on assessment and pedagogical issues.

## Enlarging the assessment community and usefulness of teacher assessment results

The emergence of an assessment community within a school can also be evaluated with reference to the extent to which schools seek to incorporate or 'enculturate' (Wiliam 1998) other teachers, pupils and their parents so that they all might share a common language and understanding of assessment. More specifically, the project sought to understand the extent to which the wider community was helped to gain a sense of the standards and quality of work required for the different levels at Key Stage 1. The interviews sought to ascertain how parents and pupils are drawn into the school's assessment processes and practices. The interviews also sought to elicit Year 2 teachers' views on the potential usefulness of their teacher assessment results for Year 3 teachers, and the Year 3 interviews sought to ascertain the use made of that information.

In relation to parents, all teachers cast themselves in the role of 'information givers' and, to varying degrees, as 'interpreters' of teacher assessment (and NCA) terminology. It would seem that mostly the communication was one way and some teachers appeared to 'protect' parents from the bureaucracy and language of assessment that they perceived would be alienating to them. Those schools where teachers themselves met to discuss teacher assessment (especially East Street and Easterly schools) went to greater lengths to make the results and the processes meaningful to parents by sharing with them examples of levelled work and by discussing the contents of their child's portfolio.

Teachers at East Street, for example, pointed out that parents understand more than in previous years: 'I think that parents here are more aware now ... at parents' evenings we will be explaining to parents what that level means and where we hope their child will be in another year, although I still think that we could do better and pass on more information'. Teachers in this school have their work with parents made more difficult by a combination of factors including non-attendance of some parents at meetings and the need to have an interpreter in the case of those parents whose first language is not English. They are, however, aware of the need to engage in dialogue with parents and they have organized displays of levelled work for scrutiny by parents.

Teachers in West Street resisted giving detailed information to parents. This comment from one Year 2 teacher in West Street was in line with those from her colleagues in this large school: 'When we have parents' evenings I will ask the parents if they want any more information. But I only really give it if they ask. It's all there for them ... but it's down to time and I haven't the time to go through all the teacher assessment with them'. Another teacher in this school confirmed: 'We have never shown samples of work'.

Differences between the schools are even sharper when considering the extent to which they attempt the enculturation (Wiliam 1998) of pupils into the assessment community. By this we mean the extent to which teachers sought to help pupils understand the criteria against which their work was judged. Once again this is linked with the opportunities teachers themselves have for debating their assessment practice. In West Street a Year 2 teacher, when asked about the possibility of using a child's portfolio of levelled work as a basis for teacher-child discussion, gave the reply: 'They're not for children. They're for staff'. In line with our analysis in Chapter 4, assessment appeared to be something that teachers do *for* children rather than *with* children. One teacher, in response to a question about helping children understand how their work is judged, said: 'I don't think they need to know very much'.

In East Street there is much more optimism about the possibility of drawing pupils into the assessment process and improving their understanding of success criteria. These teachers were beginning to see assessment as something that teachers might do with their pupils (as well as *to* them). Albeit at a quite crude and behaviourist level a number of teachers in this school talked of their attempts to communicate with pupils about the quality of their work and what they needed to do to improve it. For example, one teacher in this school talked about how she tries to help her pupils understand what they must do to improve their writing: 'As a class we look closely at an individual child's work. We might blow up a piece of writing on an OHP, read through it and then say how we can make it better'.

The assessment coordinator in this school confirmed that pupils across the school are increasingly made aware of how to improve their work and engage in self-assessment:

> We already have children setting their own targets, especially in writing and we're starting in maths. So they are becoming more aware of what they need to do to improve and how to recognize when they have done something well. They can show you evidence of achieving a target. They're beginning a little bit of self-assessment.

It appears that in only a few of our schools was there any real grasp of the importance of involving pupils in the assessment process. We have argued throughout this book for pupils to be increasingly responsible for their learning and to take an active role in assessment. Accordingly they need to be more involved in the assessment processes and practices of their schools, in the shared scrutiny of their own work and in the co-constructing of future learning steps.

## Passing on assessment information to other teachers

In every school in our study the teacher assessment results are passed on to the Year 3 teacher. As we already noted in Chapter 2, NCA policy since the mid-1990s assumes that the results of the levelling exercise should support teachers in making pedagogical decisions (Dearing 1993, 1994). Yet again, our evidence suggests that the use and usefulness of the information in this regard would appear to be linked to the involvement of the Year 3 teacher in the teacher assessment process and to the meaningfulness of the information.

However, the information passed on was, at best, seen as useful for allocating pupils to similar ability groups in the new class and, at worst, simply ignored in favour of personal judgement. It was not surprising, given the collaborative ethos of East Street, that the Year 3 teacher was positive in her appraisal of the assessment information that she received from her Year 2 colleagues. In addition to the collaboration about teacher assessment that occurred in this school, handover from the Year 2 to the Year 3 teacher meant receiving level information that she understood, trusted and was able to use. The teacher clearly felt part of the school's assessment community and understood her role within it. She said:

> I think we've got it right. This is my first year in this school and I found that the information that I got enabled me to adequately assess the children. I was able to group them by ability for various subjects on the assessments that came from Year 2. It gave me a pretty fair picture of

where they were at. And I was able also to use those assessments to set my own targets this year.

In sharp contrast, the Year 3 teacher at West Street, where collaboration about assessment was minimal, appeared to make very little use of the assessment information that was passed on to her from her Year 2 colleagues. Like many Year 3 teachers reported elsewhere (Hall *et al.* 1997) she preferred the 'fresh start' approach and felt safer with her own judgements of the children, claiming to use official end of key stage assessment as a source to consult should 'problems' arise: 'I'd like my personal judgement to take over. But it's nice to have those records to go back to if you come up against a problem'.

## Conclusion

While there is evidence of the emergence of an assessment community of practice within some schools, such communities are confined mainly to the teachers within those particular schools. The potential for both learners themselves and their parents to be more actively involved has not yet been fully explored and exploited. In addition, the lack of networking with teachers in neighbouring schools, although a feature of past assessment practice, means that the development of a community of practice could be judged to be still fragmentary.

To understand why these schools are not more advanced in this regard and why other schools are still isolationist in assessment style, it is necessary to consider the status of teacher assessment in relation to other initiatives and the consequences of this for teachers' professional learning, and to set this within the wider context of government priorities. Some of these issues were highlighted in Chapter 2.

The metaphor of the 'back burner' sums up the attitude towards teacher assessment – several teachers in several schools talked about teacher assessment processes taking 'a back seat', being put 'on hold' and being 'in the past'. They perceived teacher aassessment as not having the status it once had: as one Year 2 teacher in Westerly School said: 'I don't think teacher assessment is valued ultimately'. Some feared that the expertise that was built up in the past may be getting lost as other initiatives clamour for attention. The fact that funding was not made available for teachers to moderate their teacher assessment results served to tell teachers that the results of the external testing programme (the SATs) were prioritized over teacher assessment. In addition, the fact that the SATs, and not teacher assessment results provide the basis of target setting and league tables further reinforced this message.

Teachers in our study, in general, were becoming much more aware of the political push to raise standards. It is not surprising that considering the high stakes nature of this assessment agenda, with its published performance tables and its target setting based on SATs results, teacher assessment, which is dependent on teacher judgement, is not prioritized. The fact that teacher assessment, more than most other recent initiatives introduced into schools, depends on teachers exercising their professional judgement means that teacher professionalism is enhanced and affirmed accordingly. The diminished status of teacher assessment therefore, in more recent years, threatens that sense of professionalism.

There is abundant evidence now that the quality of teaching and learning inside the classroom is strongly influenced by the quality of the professional relationships teachers have with their colleagues outside the classroom (Hargreaves and Evans 1997; Anderson and Herr 1999). Assessment powerfully exemplifies this in England. One of the unplanned consequences of the national reforms on assessment was teachers' sophistication in assessment expertise as a result of professional collaboration and the building of professional cultures among primary teachers in the wake of the introduction of the National Curriculum and its assessment framework (Woods 1993; Gipps *et al.* 1998).

The real danger in recent years in relation to teacher assessment is that not only are such cultures or communities of assessment practice not being supported and developed, but the ground that was gained in the early and mid-1990s could have receded. However, the recent pronouncements by Secretary of State for Education and Skills, Charles Clarke, on 'excellence' and 'enjoyment' and, more particularly, the plans to reconsider assessment policy at Key Stage 1 hint at a tempering of the rigidity of the existing regime of assessment and are a step in the right direction.

# Conclusion

In recent times assessment policy in primary education in this country has been driven by demands for system accountability at the expense of the needs of learners. Yet research has shown that the kind of assessment that really matters for raising standards is assessment that yields information that learners can use to progress their own learning. In this book we have tried to support this process by exploring issues that are central to the complex task of assessing learning in a way that directly informs and supports learning. We recognize the complexity of the teacher's task in implementing formative assessment practices.

As others (e.g. Black and Wiliam 1998b; Torrance and Pryor 1998) have already shown, implementing formative assessment requires more than a mechanical attention to methods; it involves a mindset that places learners at the heart of the assessment enterprise. The implications of this mindset are that learners and teachers together describe, evaluate and set goals for learning, that together they discuss the attributes of successful products and that they begin to share notions of what constitutes quality in pupils' work. It also implies a recognition of how pupils' achievement is influenced by a host of factors, from the involvement of peers, the support of the teacher, the use of resources and the learning setting, to pupils' own commitment, engagement, persistence, prior learning and experiences, previous achievements in the learning domain in question and perceptions of the demands of the tasks set for them.

Assessment that is learning-orientated encourages pupils, teachers and other adults to recognize the partiality and contested nature of evidence of achievement. Crucially, learners help themselves to learn by having opportunities to reflect on what and how they have learned in various domains, and on what counts as evidence of success in various domains. They need multiple and varied exemplars together with constructive feedback on their own performances to help them internalize the characteristics of quality and monitor and assess their own and others' work.

This perspective of learning and assessment suggests a dialogic as opposed to monologic classroom where class time is devoted to pupil questioning, collaborative group work, peer and self-assessment and authentic talk. As Wertsch and Toma (1995: 171) explain:

> In general, it is reasonable to expect that when the dialogic function is dominant in classroom discourse, pupils will treat their utterances and those of others as thinking devices. Instead of accepting them as information to be received, encoded, and stored, they will take an active stance toward them by questioning and extending them, by incorporating them into their own internal utterances, and so forth. When the univocal function is dominant, the opposite can reasonably be expected to be the case.

This shift to the dialogic classroom may well be the most challenging aspect to accomplish in the current context of an overcrowded curriculum and heavy emphasis on external assessments. In our view, without dialogic discourse, it is unlikely that learners will maximize their own learning power and classrooms will not become communities of practice or discourse communities where pupil talk gradually comes to resemble the discourses used by working scientists, historians, readers, writers etc. (Ritchie 2001).

In the rush to measure, compare and set targets for classes, schools and LEAs, we have neglected learners' needs for assessment information that is meaningful to them in the here and now of their learning – that is, information that they can use to take the next steps in their learning. Unless our approach to assessment is working for the benefit of learners, our efforts to raise standards in other ways will remain limited. When assessments are high stakes, as in the current situation, teachers tend to adopt a teaching style that is monologic, which emphasizes transmission teaching of knowledge.

Add to this the inhibitive effect of curriculum coverage and it is not surprising that new practices are slow to get off the ground. Recent evidence shows that a transmission approach favours pupils who prefer to learn in this way and disadvantages and lowers the self-esteem of those who prefer to be more active and like creative ways of learning (Harlen and Deakin Crick 2002).

However, the beginnings of a shift away from the rigid accountability model are appearing as we complete this book. We detect some attention to learning processes. The new recognition in the *NLS* of dialogue and classroom interaction manifested in the Teaching Through Dialogue initiative, the emphasis of the Secretary of State for Education and skills on 'excellence and enjoyment', his suggestion that teacher assessment may play a greater role than currently at Key Stage 1, and the elements within the FSP all point to a tempering of the outcomes and system accountability model. In addition, the greater emphasis in Ofsted inspections on formative assessment in general supports our cautious optimism. While these shifts are certainly in the right direction, they still fall short of the level of assessment sophistication needed. There remains an overemphasis on assessment as measurement and a reluctance to recognize assessment as about judgement. What is certain is that assessment policies and practices need to be in line with current understanding of the nature of learners, learning and knowledge.

# References

Alexander, R. (2000) *Culture and Pedagogy: International Comparisons in Primary Education*. Oxford: Blackwell.

Allal, L. (2002) The assessment of learning dispositions in the classroom, *Assessment in Education*, 9(1): 55–8.

Allington, R.L. and Johnston, P.H. (2001) What do we know about effective 4th grade teachers and their teaching? in C. Roller (ed.) *Learning to Teach Reading: Setting the Research Agenda*. Newark, DE: International Reading Association.

Anderson, G.L. and Herr, K. (1999) The new paradigm wars: is there room for rigorous practitioner knowledge in schools and universities? *Educational Researcher*, 28(5): 12–21.

Arnold, H. (1982) *Listening to Children Reading*. London: Hodder & Stoughton.

Au, K.H. (1994) Portfolio assessment: experiences at the Kamehameha Elementary Education Program (KEEP), in S.W. Valencia, E.H. Hiebert and P.P. Afflerbach (eds) *Authentic Reading Assessment: Practices and Possibilities*, 103–126. Newark, DE: International Reading Association.

Au, K.H. (1997) A sociocultural model of reading instruction: the Kamehameha Elementary Education Program, in S.A. Stahl (ed.) *Instructional Models in Reading*, 181–202. Hillsdale, NJ: Lawrence Erlbaum.

Au, K.H., Carroll, J.H. and Scheu, J.A. (1997) *Balanced Literacy Instruction: A Teacher's Resource Book*. Norwood, MA: Christopher Gordon.

Bage, G. (2000) *Thinking History 4–14*. London: Routledge-Falmer.

Bakhtin, M. (1981) *The Dialogic Imagination*. Austin, TX: University of Texas Press.

Barber, M. (1996) *The Learning Game*. London: Victor Gollancz.

Barnes, D. (1989) *Knowledge as Action*, in P. Murphyand and B. Moon (eds) *Developments in Learning and Assessment*. London: Hodder & Stoughton.

Barrs, M., Ellis, S., Hester, H. and Thomas, A. (1990) *The Primary Language Record*. London: Centre for Language in Primary Education.

Bernstein, B. (1996) *Pedagogy, Symbolic Control and Identity: Theory, Research, Critique*. London: Taylor & Francis.

Black, P. (1997) Whatever happened to TGAT? in C. Cullingford (ed.) *Assessment Versus Evaluation*, 24–50. London: Cassell.

Black, P. (1999) Assessment, learning theories and testing systems, in P. Murphy (ed.) *Learners, Learning and Assessment*, 118–34. London: Paul Chapman.

Black, P. and Wiliam, D. (1998a) *Inside the Black Box*. London: King's College.

Black, P. and Wiliam, D. (1998b) Assessment and classroom learning, *Assessment in Education*, 5(1): 7–84.

Black, P. and Wiliam, D. (2001) Theory and practice in the development of formative assessment. Paper presented at the ninth biennial conference of the European Association for Learning and Instruction, University of Freiburg, Switzerland, August.

Blatchford, P. (2003) *The Class Size Debate: Is Small Better?* Buckingham: Open University Press.

Blatchford, P., Baines, E., Kutnick, P. and Martin, C. (2001) Classroom contexts: connections between class size and within class groupings, *British Journal of Educational Psychology*, 71(2): 283–302.

Blenkin, G. and Kelly, V. (eds) (1992) *Assessment in Early Childhood Education.* London: Paul Chapman.

Broadfoot, P.M. (1996) *Education, Assessment and Society: A Sociological Analysis.* Buckingham: Open University Press.

Broadfoot, P.M. (1999) Empowerment or performativity? English assessment policy in the late twentieth century. Paper presented at the Assessment Reform Group Symposium on Assessment Policy, Univeristy of Brighton.

Broks, P. (2003) *Into the Silent Land: Travels in Neuropsychology.* London: Atlantic Books.

Brophy, J. and VanSledright, B. (1997) *Teaching and Learning History in Elementary Schools.* New York: Teachers College Press.

Brown, A. and Ferrara, R. (1985) Diagnosing zones of proximal development, in J. Wertsch (ed.) *Culture, Communication and Cognition: Vygotskian Perspectives,* 273–305. Cambridge: Cambridge University Press.

Bruner, J. (1986) *Actual Mind Possible Worlds.* Cambridge, MA: Harvard University Press.

Bruner, J. (1989) The transactional self, in P. Murphy and B. Moon (eds) *Development in Learning and Assessment,* 37–48. London: Hodder & Stoughton.

Bruner, J. (1990) *Acts of Meaning.* Cambridge, MA: Harvard University Press.

Bruner, J. (1996) *The Culture of Education.* Cambridge, MA: Harvard University Press.

Burke, W.M. (2000a) Journeying beyond models and typologies: towards a better understanding of formative assessment for learning. EdD thesis, The Open University.

Burke, W.M. (2000b) Journeying beyond models and typologies: a constructivist view of classroom assessment. Paper presented at the BERA Conference, Cardiff, September.

Burningham, J. (1977) *Come Away from the Water, Shirley.* London: Collins.

Calfee, R. (1996) Review essay, carts, horses and rollercoasters, in C.V. Gipps (ed.) Beyond testing: towards a theory of educational assessment, *Assessment in Education,* 3(1): 99–104.

Callaghan, J. (1987) *Time and Chance.* London: Collins.

Calouste Gulbenkian Foundation (1982) *The Arts in Schools.* Calouste Gulbenkian Foundation.

Carr, M. (1999) Being a learner: five learning dispositions for early childhood, *Early Childhood Practice*, 1(1): 81–99.

Carr, M. (2001) *Assessment in Early Childhood Settings*. London: Paul Chapman.

Carr, M. and Claxton, G. (2002) Tracking the development of learning dispositions, *Assessment in Education*, 9(1): 9–37.

Carr, M. and May, H. (1993) Choosing a model: reflecting on the development process of Te Whariki: national early childhood curriculum guidelines in New Zealand, *International Journal of Early Years Education*, 1(3): 7–21.

Claxton, G. (1995) What kind of learning does self-assessment drive? Developing a 'nose' for quality; comments on Klenowski, *Assessment in Education*, 2: 339–43.

Claxton, G. (1999) *Wise Up: The Challenge of Lifelong Learning*. London: Bloomsbury.

Clay, M. (1985) *The Early Detection of Reading Difficulties*, 3rd edn. London: Heinemann.

Cole, M. (1990) Cognitive development and formal schooling, in L. Moll (ed.) *Vygotsky and Education*, 89–110. New York: Cambridge University Press.

Cowie, B. and Bell, B. (1999) A model of formative assessment in science education, *Assessment in Education*, 6(1): 101–16.

Darling-Hammond, L., Ancess, J. and Falk, B. (1995) *Authentic Assessment in Action*. New York: Teachers College Press.

Daugherty, R. (1995) *National Curriculum Assessment: A Review of Policy 1987–1994*. London: Falmer Press.

Daugherty, R. (1997) Consistency in teachers' assessments: defining the problem, finding the answers, *British Journal of Curriculum and Assessment*, 8(1): 32–8.

Dearing, R. (1993) *The National Curriculum and its Assessment: An Interim Report*. London: SCAA.

Dearing, R. (1994) *The National Curriculum and its Assessment: Final Report*. London: SCAA.

Deci, E.L. and Ryan, R.M. (1994) Promoting self-determined education, *Scandinavian Journal of Educational Research*, 58: 438–81.

Denvir, B. (1989) Assessment purposes and learning in mathematics education, in P. Murphy and B. Moon (eds) *Developments in Learning and Assessment*, 277–90. London: Hodder & Stoughton.

DES (Department of Education and Science) (1985) *Better Schools*. London: HMSO.

DES (Department of Education and Science) (1988) *Task Group on Assessment and Testing: A Report*. London: HMSO.

Dewey, J. (1934) *Art as Experience*. New York: Minton, Balch & Company.

DfE (Department for Education) (1995) *History in the National Curriculum*. London: HMSO.

DfEE (Department For Education and Employment) (1998) *The National Literacy Strategy*. Cambridge: Cambridge University Press.

DfEE (Department For Education and Employment) (1999) *The National Numeracy Strategy*. Cambridge: Cambridge University Press.

DfEE (Department for Education and Employment) (2001) *The NNS: The First Year*. London: DfEE.

DfEE (Department for Education and Skills) (2003) *Excellence and Enjoyment: A Strategy for Primary Schools*. Nottingham: DfES.

Dickinson, A.K. and Lee, P.J. (1984) Making sense of history, in A. Dickinson, P. Lee and R. Rogers (eds) *Learning History*, 117–53. London: Heinemann.

Dillon, J.T. (1985) Using questions to foil discussion, *Teaching and Teacher Education*, 1(2): 109–21.

Donmoyer, R. (1995) A knowledge base for educational administration: notes from the field, in R. Donmoyer, M. Imber and J. Scheurich (eds) *The Knowledge Base in Educational Administration: Multiple Perspectives*, 74–95. Albany, NY: SUNY Press.

Drummond, M.J. (1999) Baseline assessment: a case for civil disobedience? in C. Conner (ed.) *Assessment in Action in the Primary School*, 3–49. London: Falmer Press.

Duffy, G. and Roehler, L.R. (1993) *Improving Classroom Reading Instruction: A Decision-making Approach*. New York: McGraw-Hill.

Duffy, G., Roehler, L. and Herrmann, G. (1988) Modelling mental processes helps poor readers become strategic readers, *The Reading Teacher*, 41: 762–7.

Dweck, C. (1986) Motivational processes affecting learning, *American Psychologist*, special issue, *Psychological Science and Education*, 41: 1040–8.

Dweck, C. (1989) Motivation, in A. Lesgold and R. Glaser (eds) *Foundations for a Psychology of Education*. Hillsdale, NJ: Lawrence Erlbaum.

Dweck, C. (1999) Caution – praise can be dangerous, *American Educator*, 23(1): 4–9.

Dweck, C. and Leggett, E. (1988) A social-cognitive approach to motivation and personality, *Psychological Review*, 95: 256–73.

Dyson, A.H. (1997) *Writing Superheroes: Contemporary Childhood, Popular Culture and Classroom Literacy*. New York: Teachers College Press.

Eisner, E. (1985) *The Art of Educational Evaluation: A Personal View*. Lewes: Falmer Press.

Falk, B. (1998) Using direct evidence to assess student progress: how the Primary Language Record supports teaching and learning, in C. Harrison and T. Salinger (eds) *Assessing Reading: Theory and Practice*, 152–65. London: Routledge.

Filer, A. and Pollard, A. (2000) *The Social World of Pupil Assessment: Processes and Contexts of Primary Schooling*. London: Continuum.

Fines, J. (1994) Progression: a seminar report, *Teaching History*, 75: 27–8.

Frederiksen, J.R. and Collins, A. (1989) A systems approach to educational testing, *Educational Researcher*, 18: 27–32.

Frederiksen, J.R. and White, B.J. (1997) Reflective assessment of students' research within an inquiry-based middle school science curriculum, in *Proceedings of Annual Meeting of the AERA Conference*, Chicago.

Freire, P. (1989) The politics of education, in P. Murphyand and B. Moon (eds)

*Developments in Learning and Assessment*, 48–55. London: Hodder & Stoughton.

Fullan, M. (1989) Planning, doing and coping with change, in P. Murphy and B. Moon (eds) *Policies for the Curriculum*, 183–212. London: Hodder & Stoughton.

Garner, R. (1987) *Metacognition and Reading Comprehension*. Mahwah, NJ: Ablex Publishing Corporation.

Gipps, C. (1994a) *Beyond Testing: Towards a Theory of Educational Assessment*. London: Falmer Press.

Gipps, C. (1994b) Developments in educational assessment: what makes a good test? *Assessment in Education*, 1(3): 283–91.

Gipps, C. and Goldstein, H. (1983) *Monitoring Children: An Evaluation for the Assessment of Performance Unit*. London: Heinemann Educational Books.

Gipps, C. and Murphy, P. (1994) *A Fair Test Assessment: Achievement and Equity*. Buckingham: Open University Press.

Gipps, C., Brown, M., McCallum, B. and McAlister, S. (1995) *Intuition or Evidence? Teachers and National Assessment of Seven Year Olds*. Buckingham: Open University Press.

Gipps, C., Clarke, S. and McCallum, B. (1998) The role of teachers in national assessment in England. Paper presented at the American Educational Research Association Conference, Chicago, April.

Glaser, B.G. and Strauss, A.L. (1967) *The Discovery of Grounded Theory*. London: Weidenfeld & Nicholson.

Goleman, D. (1995) *Emotional Intelligence*. New York: Bantam.

Good, T.J. and Brophy, J.E. (1994) *Looking in Classrooms*, 6th edn. New York: Harper Collins College Publishers.

Goodman, K.S. (1973) Miscues: windows on the reading process, in F.V. Gollash (ed.) (1982) *Language and Literacy: The Selected Writings of Kenneth S. Goodman, Process, Theory, Research 1*. London: Routledge & Kegan Paul.

Goodman, Y.M., Watson, D. and Burke, C. (1987) *Reading Miscue Analysis: Alternative Strategies*. New York: Richard C. Owen.

Graves, D. (1991) Build a Literacy Classroom. Portsmouth, NH: Heinemann.

Greene, M. (1994) The arts and national standards, *The Educational Forum*, 58 (summer): 391–400.

Hall, K. (1995) Learning modes: an investigation of pupils in five Kent classrooms, *Educational Research*, 37(1): 21–32.

Hall, K. (2002) Co-constructing subjectivities and knowledge in literacy class: an ethnographic-sociocultural perspective, *Language and Education*, 16 (1): 178–94.

Hall, K. (2003) *Listening to Stephen Read: Multiple Perspectives on Literacy*. Buckingham: Open University Press.

Hall, K. and Harding, A. (1999) Teacher assessment of seven year olds in England: a study of its summative function, *Early Years International Journal of Research and Development*, 20(2): 19–28.

Hall, K. and Harding, A. (2002) Level descriptions and teacher assessment: towards a community of assessment practice, *Educational Research*, 40(1): 1–16.

Hall, K. and Harding, A. (2003) A Systematic Review of Effective Literacy Teaching in the 4–14 Age Range of Mainstream Schooling: In *Research Evidence in Eduation Library*. London: EPPI-Centre, Social Science Research Unit Institute of Education.

Hall, K., Webber, B., Varley, S., Young, V. and Dorman, P. (1997) A study of teacher assessment at Key Stage One, *Cambridge Journal of Education*, 27(1): 107–22.

Hall, K., Myers, J. and Bowman, H. (1999) Tasks, texts and contexts: a study of metacognition and reading in English and Irish primary classrooms, *Educational Studies*, 25(2): 311–25.

Hall, K., Allan, C., Dean, J. and Warren, S. (in press) Classroom discourse in the Literacy Hour in England, *Language, Culture and Curriculum*.

Hallden, O. (1994) On the paradox of understanding history in an educational setting, in G. Leinhardt, I. Beck and C. Stainton (eds) *Teaching and Learning in History*, 27–46. Hillsdale, NJ: Lawrence Erlbaum.

Halsey, A.H. and Gardener, L. (1953) Selection for secondary education, *British Journal of Sociology*, 1(5): 4–7.

Hargreaves, A. and Evans, R. (1997) *Beyond Educational Reform: Bringing Teachers Back In*. Buckingham: Open University Press.

Harlen, W. and Deakin Crick, R. (2002) A systematic review of the impact of summative assessment and tests on students' motivation for learning, EPPI-Centre Review, version 1.1, in *Research Evidence in Education*. London: EPPI-Centre, Social Science Research Unit, Institute of Education.

Harlen, W. and James, M. (1997) Assessment and learning: differences and relationships between formative and summative assessment, *Assessment in Education*, 4(3): 365–79.

Harrison, C., Bailey, M. and Foster, C. (1998) Responsive assessment of reading: seeking evidence on reading attainment from students, in M. Coles and R. Jenkins (eds) *Assessing Reading 2: Changing Practice in Classrooms*. London: Routledge.

Hicks, D. (2001) Literacies and masculinities in the life of a young working-class boy, *Language Arts*, 78(3): 217–26.

Hirsch, E.D. Jr. (1987) *Cultural Literacy*. New York: Vantage.

Holt, J. (1965) *How Children Fail*. London: Pitman.

Hoodless, P. (2002) An investigation into children's developing awareness of time and chronology in story, *Journal of Curriculum Studies*, 34(2): 173–200.

Hoyle, C. (1989) What is the point of group discussion in mathematics? in P. Murphy and B. Moon (eds) *Policies for the Curriculum*. London: Hodder & Stoughton.

James, M. and Gipps, C. (1998) Broadening the basis of assessment to prevent the narrowing of learning, *The Curriculum Journal*, 9(3): 285–97.

Johnston, P.H. (1992) *Constructive Evaluation of Literate Activity*. New York: Longman.

Katz, L. (2002) Not all dispositions are desirable: implications for assessment, *Assessment in Education*, 9(1): 53–4.

Klenowski, V. (2002) Developing Portfolios for Learning and Assessment. London: Routledge Falmer

Kluger, A.N. and De Nisi, A. (1996) The effects of feedback interventions on performance: a historical review, a meta-analysis and a preliminary feedback intervention theory, *Psychological Bulletin*, 119: 254–84.

Knight, P. (1991) Teaching as exposure: the case of good practice in junior school history, *British Educational Research Journal*, 17: 76–85.

Kolb, D.A. (1984) *Experiential Learning: Experience on the Source of Learning and Development*. Englewood Cliffs, NJ: Prentice Hall.

Krechersky, M. (1991) Project spectrum: an innovative assessment alternative, *Educational Leadership*, 48(5): 43–9.

Kreisberg, S. (1992) *Transforming Power: Domination, Empowerment and Education*. New York: State University of New York Press.

Lawlor, S. (1989) Correct core, in B. Moon, P. Murphy and J. Raynor (eds) *Policies For The Curriculum*, 58–70. London: Hodder & Stoughton.

Lawton, D. (1992) Whatever happened to the TGAT report? In C. Gipps (ed.) *Developing Assessment for National Curriculum*. London: Kogan Page/ULIE.

Lawton, D. (1994) *The Tory Mind on Education 1979–1994*. London: Falmer Press.

Lee, P. and Smagorinsky, P. (eds) (2000) *Vygotskian Perspectives on Literacy Research*. Cambridge: Cambridge University Press.

Lee, P., Dickinson, A. and Ashby, R. (1996) There were no facts in those days: children's ideas about historical explanation, in M. Hughes (ed.) *Teaching and Learning in Changing Times*. Oxford: Blackwell.

Leont'ev, A. (1981) *Problems of the Development of the Mind*. Moscow: Progress Publishers.

Leshe, L. and Jett-Simpson, M. (1997) *Authentic Literacy Assessment: An Ecological Approach*. New York: Longman.

Madaus, G.F. (1994) A technological and historical consideration of equity issues associated with proposals to change the nation's testing policy, *Harvard Education Review*, 64(1): 76–5.

Marsland, D. and Seaton, N. (1993) *The Empire Strikes Back: The Creative Subversion of the National Curriculum*. York: Campaign for Real Education.

May, H. and Carr, M. (2000) Empowering children to learn and grow – Te Whariki: The New Zealand early childhood national curriculum, in J. Hayden (ed.) *Landscapes in Early Childhood Education*, 153–69. New York: Peter Lang.

Mercer, N. (1995) *The Guided Construction of Knowledge*. Clevedon, MA: Multilingual Matters.

Modbury County Primary School (1990) National Curriculum Record Book. Modbury: Modbury Marketing Ltd.

Moon, C. (1990) Miscue made simple, *Child Education*, November.

Munby, S. *et al.* (1989) *Assessing and Recording Achievement*. London: Blackwell.

Murphy, P. (1989) Gender and assessment in science, in P. Murphy and B. Moon (eds) *Developments in Learning and Assessment*, 323–37. London: Hodder & Stoughton.

Murphy, S., Shannon, P., Johnston, P. and Hansen, J. (1998) *Fragile Evidence: A Critique of Reading Assessment*. Mahwah, NJ: Lawrence Erlbaum.

Nichol, J. with Dean, J. (1997) *History 7–11: Developing Primary Teaching Skills*. London: Routledge.

Nuttall, D. (1987) The validity of assessments, *European Journal of the Psychology of Education*, 11(2): 109–18.

Nuttall, D.L. (1989) The validity of assessment, in P. Murphy and B. Moon (eds) *Policies For The Curriculum*, 265–76. London: Hodder & Stoughton.

Nystrand, M., Wu, L.L., Gamoran, A., Zeiser, S. and Long, D. (2001) *Questions in Time: Investigating the Structure and Dynamics of Unfolding Classroom Discourse*, Report 14005 from the Center on English Learning and Achievement (CELA), http:cela.albany.edu/nystrand01–5/main.htm.l

Ofsted (Office for Standards in Education) (1999) *Guidance on the Inspection of Nursery and Primary Schools with Guidance on Self-evaluation, Effective from January 2000*. London: HMSO.

Ogle, D. (1986) K-W-L: a teaching model that develops active reading of expository text, *The Reading Teacher*, 39: 564–70.

O'Sullivan, J. and Joy, R. (1994) If at first you don't succeed: children's metacognition about reading problems, *Contemporary Educational Psychology*, 19: 118–27.

Perrenoud, P. (1998) From formative evaluation to a controlled regulation of learning processes: towards a wider conceptual field, *Assessment in Education*, 5(1): 85–102.

Piaget, J. (1972) *Psychology and Epistemology*. Harmondsworth: Penguin.

Plowden Report (1967) *Children and their Primary Schools*. London: Central Advisory Council.

Podmore, V. and Carr, M. (1999) Learning and teaching stories: new approaches to assessment and evaluation. Paper presented at the Australian Association for Research in Education, New Zealand Association for Research in Education (AARE-NZARE), Melbourne, December.

Pollard, A. and Filer, A. (1996) *The Social World of Children's Learning: Case Studies of Pupils from Four to Seven*. London: Cassell.

Project Zero and Reggio Children (2001) *Making Learning Visible: Children as Individual and Group Learners*. Reggio Emilia, Italy: Reggio Children.

Purves, A. (1993) Setting standards in the language arts and literature classroom and the implications for portfolio assessment, *Educational Assessment*, 1(3): 175–99.

QCA (Qualifications and Curriculum Authority) (2003) *Foundation Stage Profile*

*Handbook,* http://www.qca.org.uk/ca/foundation/profiles.asp, accessed 10 June 2003.

QCA (Qualifications and Curriculum Authority)/DfEE (Department for Education and Employment) (2000) *Curriculum Guidance for the Foundation Stage.* London: HMSO.

Raynor, J. (1989) *Curriculum Chronologies, England and Wales,* in B. Moon, P. Murphy and J. Raynor (eds) *Policies For The Curriculum.* London: Hodder & Stoughton.

Ritchie, S.M. (2001) Actions and discourses for transformative understanding in a middle school science class, *International Journal of Science Education,* 23(3): 283–99.

Roach, J. (1971) *Public Examinations in England 1850–1906.* Cambridge: Cambridge University Press.

Roehler, L.R. and Cantlon, D.J. (1996) *Scaffolding: a powerful tool in social constructivist classrooms,* http://www.ntu.edu.au/education/ntier/newsletter/scaffolding.html.

Ross, M., Radnor, H., Mitchell, S. and Brierton, C. (1993) *Assessing Achievement in the Arts.* Buckingham: Open University Press.

Sadler, D.R. (1989) Formative assessment and the design of instructional systems, *Instructional Science,* 18: 119–44.

Sadler, D.R. (1998) Formative assessment: revisiting the territory, *Assessment in Education,* 5: 77–84.

Salomon, G. (ed.) (1993) *Introduction Distributed Cognitions: Psychological and Educational Considerations.* Cambridge: Cambridge University Press.

Sansom, C. (1987) Concepts, skills and content: a developmental approach to the history syllabus, in C. Portal (ed.) *The History Curriculum for Teachers,* 116–41. London: Falmer.

Scribner, S. and Cole, M. (1973) Cognitive consequences of formal and informal education, *Science,* 182: 553–9.

Sendak, M. (1988) *Where the Wild Things Are.* London: HarperCollins.

Sfard, A. (1998) On two metaphors for learning and the dangers of choosing just one, *Educational Researcher,* 27(2): 4–13.

Shepard, L.A. (2000) The role of assessment in a learning culture. Presidential address at the annual meeting of the American Educational Research Association, New Orleans, April.

Shipman, M. (1983) *Assessment in Primary and Middle Schools.* Beckenham: Croom Helm.

Simon, B. (1953) *Intelligence Testing and the Comprehensive School.* London: Lawrence & Wishart.

Sinclair, J. and Coulthard, R. (1975) *Towards an Analysis of Discourse.* London: Oxford University Press.

Smiley, P. and Dweck, C. (1994) Individual differences in achievement goals among young children, *Child Development,* 65: 6.

Sutherland, G. (1977) The magic of measurement: mental testing in education 1900–1940, *Transactions of the Royal Historical Society*, 135–53.

Tanner, H. and Jones, S. (1994) Using peer and pupil self-assessment to develop modelling skills with students aged 11–16: a socioconstructive view, *Educational Studies in Mathematics*, 27: 413–31.

Taylor, B.M., Pearson, P.D. *et al.* (2000) Effective schools and accomplished teachers: lessons about primary-grade reading instruction in low-income schools, *Elementary School Journal*, 101(2): 121–65.

The Open University (1990) *E819 Curriculum, Learning and Assessment*, Section 7. Milton Keynes: The Open University.

Thomas, N. (1990) *Primary Education from Plowden to the 1990s*. Basingstoke: Falmer Press.

Tierney, R. (1998) Literacy assessment reform: shifting beliefs, principled possibilities, and emerging practices, *The Reading Teacher*, 51(5): 374–90.

Tompkins, G.E. (1997) *Literacy for the 21st Century: A Balanced Approach*. Upper Saddle River, NJ: Prentice Hall.

Torrance, H. and Pryor, J. (1998) *Investigating Formative Assessment, Teaching, Learning and Assessment in the Classroom*. Buckingham: Open University Press.

Tunstall, P. and Gipps, C. (1996) Teacher feedback to young children in formative assessment: a typology, *British Educational Research Journal*, 22(4): 389–404.

Turner, T. and Krechevsky, M. (2003) Project Spectrum/Reggio Emilia: who are the teachers? Who are the learners? *Educational Leadership*, April: 40–3.

Tyler, R.W. (1949) *Basic Principles of Curriculum and Instruction*. Chicago: University of Chicago Press.

Valencia, S.W. (1990) A portfolio approach to classroom reading assessment: the whys, whats, and hows, *Reading Teacher*, 43: 338–40.

Valencia, S.W. (1998) *Literacy Portfolios in Action*. Texas: Harcourt Brace.

Valencia, S.W. and Place, N.A. (1994) Literacy portfolios for teaching, learning, and accountability: the Bellevue Literacy Assessment Project, in S.W. Valencia, E.H. Hiebert and P.P. Afflerback (eds) *Authentic Reading Assessment: Practices and Possibilities*, 134–56. Newark, DE: International Reading Association.

Vernon, P. (1957) *Secondary School Selection*. London: Methuen.

Verrier, R. (1997) *Teaching Key Stage 1 History*. Oxford: Heinemann.

von Glasersfeld, E. (1987) Learning as a constructivist activity, in C. Jenner (ed.) *Problems of Representation in Teaching and Learning Mathematics*. Hillsdale, NJ: Lawrence Erlbaum.

von Glasersfeld, E. (1989) Learning as a constructive activity, in P. Murphy and B. Moon (eds) *Developments in Learning and Assessment*, 5–18. London: Hodder & Stoughton.

Vygotsky, L. (1978) *Mind in Society: The Development of Higher Psychological Processes*. Cambridge, MA: Harvard University Press.

Vygotsky, L.S. (1987) *The Collected Works of L.S. Vygotsky*, vol. 1. New York: Plenum.

Walling, D.R. (2000) *Rethinking How Art is Taught. A Critical Convergence.* Thousand Oaks, CA: Corwin Press.

Watts, M. and Bentley, D. (1989) Constructivism in the classroom: enabling conceptual change by word and deed, in P. Murphy and B. Moon (eds) *Developments in Learning and Assessment.* London: Hodder & Stoughton.

Wertsch, J.V. and Toma, C. (1995) Discourse and learning in the classroom: a socio-cultural approach, in L.P. Steffe and J. Gale (eds) *Constructivism in Education,* 159–74. Hillsdale, NJ: Lawrence Erlbaum.

White, J. and Gorman, T. (1989) APU Language Assessment, some practical consequences of a functionally oriented approach, in P. Murphy and B. Moon (eds) *Developments in Learning and Assessment.* London: Hodder & Stoughton.

Wigfield, A., Eccles, J. and Rodriquez, D. (1998) The development of children's motivation in school contexts, *Review of Research in Education,* 23: 73–117.

Wiliam, D. (1998) Enculturating learners into communities of practice: raising achievement through classroom assessment. Paper presented at the European Conference on Educational Research (ECER), Ljubljana, Slovenia, September.

Wiliam, D. and Black, P.J. (1996) Meanings and consequences: a basis for distinguishing formative and summative functions of assessment? *British Education Research Journal,* 22: 537–48.

Wood, D. (1988) *How Children Think and Learn.* Oxford: Blackwell.

Wood, R. (1987) *Measurement and Assessment in Education and Psychology.* Lewes: Falmer Press.

Woods, P. (1993) *Critical Events in Teaching and Learning.* London: Falmer Press.

Wray, D. (1994) *Literacy and Awareness.* London: Hodder & Stoughton.

Zahorik, J. (1995) *Constructivist Teaching (Fastback 390).* Bloomington, IN: Phi Delta Kappa Educational Foundation.

# Index

# INTERACTIVE TEACHING IN THE PRIMARY SCHOOL
## Digging Deeper into Meanings

### Janet Moyles, Linda Hargreaves, Roger Merry, Fred Paterson and Veronica Esarte-Sarries

- What is 'interactive teaching' in primary classrooms?
- What do primary teachers and children do to interact effectively?
- Are there benefits in such interactions to both teaching and learning?

A research partnership of tutors and teachers strives towards answers to these key questions. This book is the story of this intriguing and exciting research project.

The authors examine the practical and theoretical aspects that are key to understanding and undertaking interactive teaching in primary classrooms. The project is unique in using its own interactive processes, 'Reflective Dialogues', to help teachers make sense of their own teaching. This process includes capturing and analysing classroom sessions on video; and cameos of these classroom interactions are discussed throughout the book. The research context is the Literacy Hour in Key Stages 1 and 2.

This new title is key reading for academics, researchers, teacher educators, policymakers and primary school teachers.

### Contents
*Acknowledgements – Foreword – Glossary – Introduction: just what is interactive teaching? – Scuppering discussion?: interaction in theory and practice – Interactive teaching: a cause for concern? – It's what I've always done!: teachers' knowledge of interactive teaching – Scratching the surface: the typology of interactive teaching I – Digging deeper into meanings: the typology of interactive teaching II – Teacher-pupil interaction and interactive teaching: synonymous or speculative? – Teachers' voices: case studies from the SPRINT project – It wasn't as bad as I thought!: learning from reflective dialogues – Can we talk about that later?: the tensions and conflicts of teaching interactively in the literacy hour – Interactive teaching: digging even deeper into meanings – References – Appendices – Index.*

224pp     0 335 21213 1 (Paperback)     0 335 21214 X (Hardback)